From Havoc to
HARMONY

—————— *5 Steps* ——————
to Restore Peace at Home
and Rebuild Your
Relationship
with Your <u>ADHD</u> Child

Gelena Gorelik

BALBOA.
PRESS
A DIVISION OF HAY HOUSE

Balboa Press books may be ordered through booksellers or by contacting:

Balboa Press
A Division of Hay House
1663 Liberty Drive
Bloomington, IN 47403
www.balboapress.com
1 (877) 407-4847

Print information available on the last page.

ISBN: 978-1-9822-2981-8 (sc)
ISBN: 978-1-9822-2983-2 (hc)
ISBN: 978-1-9822-2982-5 (e)

Library of Congress Control Number: 2019908130

Balboa Press rev. date: 10/31/2019

To my children, Abi and Sam, with all my love

Contents

Foreword by Tamra Skye

While reading this book, I was both delighted with what I was seeing and concerned.

Delighted because it's rare to see something that so closely describes the approaches I applied in both my own parenting and my years of working with at-risk youth in the classroom. Gelena's techniques—when done right—work better than any other approach I have seen.

But I was also concerned, because I know how hard it is to get buy-in from educators and parents at first. You need to be open to these ideas, and you need to apply them as consistently as possible. And you will likely stumble at first; it is very easy to fall into old patterns, undoing any progress made.

But progress can be made.

At one point in the book, Gelena gives an example of a difficult conversation between a parent and a teenager, and this illustrates a situation ripe for communication breakdown and conflict. Most people looking at this conversation will wonder how to respond to it. My answer: establish a relationship and a parenting approach that prevents this type of conversation from happening to begin with. And if you are already having this type of conversation, know that it will take time to reprogram both you and your kid. Get clear on the end goals—the real goals—and keep them in mind.

Most parents really have two main goals for their kid: to be as self-sufficient as possible and to be happy. Every other goal they might list is usually a means to one or both of these things. Unfortunately, many people get stuck on the means to the point of destroying the goals.

Are you focused on the goals, or are you stuck on the means to the goals?

For example, some think a college education is a goal, but it is only a means. People used to ask me if it bothered me that my youngest daughter took a more vocational route instead of aiming for a university degree. And why should this bother me? She enjoys her job and can make more money than most people with degrees. She also has time for fun and meaningful activities outside of work. She even bought a house at age twenty. She's very self-sufficient and happy. Goals met!

My oldest was put into special education in first grade but started college at age fourteen and has traveled half the country now "for research purposes." She's a professional writer, which allows her to make a living from one rabbit hole after another. She is as self-sufficient as possible (utilizing resources) and happy. Goals met!

These two very different kids have one thing in common: I parented them as individuals using the techniques that Gelena describes. I realized that I was doing more than raising kids; I was raising future autonomous adults. I have a wonderful relationship with these two women I raised. But wow, was it a rough ride at times! I did my best figuring things out, but not without some missteps along the way that I later had to correct for.

Not only did I have to learn how to parent in ways very different from how I was raised, I had to deal with all the naysayers in my local community. Self-doubt could rise up at any time, and even when I was very sure of what I was doing, it was a lonely road. As I was reading Gelena's steps, I found myself wishing that I'd had a coach like her. How much better would it have been with that support?

And parents need support. Our own self-care is important! Our well-being through this whole process (which includes the here and now) is essential. And that right there is what Gelena includes in her coaching that I took a lot longer to learn. While raising your kids, you need to continue nurturing yourself and your own personal goals. You do this for yourself, and you do this to model for your kids.

With that in mind, be open to the possibilities. Each step Gelena presents builds upon the previous one. As noted in the title, over time, you can move from havoc to harmony.

About Tamra Skye

Tamra is an education strategist specializing in learner-centric instructional design and clear goal-oriented project planning. Tamra has created and overhauled several education programs, including fully accredited schools; spearheaded projects like the Empowerment Community for trauma recovery; and overseen the instructional design process for projects through Open Path Studio.

Tamra's current focus areas are philosophy of perception, neurodiversity advocacy, and professional development for educators—including parents who are homeschooling or supplementing their children's education. To learn more about Tamra and read her published articles and recorded webinars, please visit TamraSkye.com or https://www.linkedin.com/in/tamraexcell/.

From the Editor by Russ Womack

The best way to learn is through experience. Sometimes life takes us through seasons of hardship and chaos, often off-guard, and always without explanation as to why. We find ourselves in the midst of something unfamiliar, and we're scared, feeling our way through the dark, making adjustments at every corner, until one day a ray of light illuminates everything we didn't see, everything we didn't know, and we find ourselves accepting all we didn't ask for. The season has exhaled. Most people choose to stop there, and understandably so—the journey, the toil, was difficult, too much at moments, and it's time for much-needed rest.

Author Gelena Gorelik found herself questioning how to raise her daughter who has ADHD. But Gelena didn't rest; instead, she made it her mission to take what she learned through that experience and find a way—a better way—to raise children and teens with ADHD. *From Havoc to Harmony* is the result of Gelena's passion and love for parents and children alike who are at different stages in their personal walk. It's a map, a blueprint, to help you find your way through the pandemonium. It allows your uncertainties to subside and your confidence to rise. She invites you to walk alongside her as she compassionately empowers you with tools and tips on how to best parent, restore peace at home, and build your relationship with your child.

It was an honor for me to edit her book. I learned new, creative, and exciting ways to parent my own children. I now see parenting from a completely different perspective and purpose, and I'm grateful to Gelena for revealing that to me.

The next best thing to learning from experience is to learn from someone who has breathed in that experience and has come out empowered with purpose and passion. Gelena Gorelik's *From Havoc to Harmony* offers exactly that.

About Russ Womack

Russ Womack lives in Prescott, Arizona, with his three kids: Max, Ethan, and Ellie. He holds a bachelor of arts degree in English from California State University, Northridge, and a bachelor of arts degree in theology from Life Christian University.

Russ has a passion for changing the way some people place shame, guilt, and condemnation on those who have committed suicide and upon the surviving loved ones. His mom committed suicide when he was twelve, and thirty-seven years later, he wrote the novel *Orange* to shine a graceful and forgiving light upon those who are hurting and have lost hope—those who believe they're unlovable, unforgivable, and unworthy. To learn more about Russ Womack and *Orange*, please visit https://www.amazon.com/Orange-Russ-Womack/dp/1542367263.

Introduction

There is no such thing as a perfect parent, so just be a real one.
—Sue Atkins

I can't believe she just said that to me. That hurts so much!

I will not cry. I don't want to cry, but the treacherous tears defy the titanic efforts of my willpower and start rolling down my face. I feel completely hopeless, helpless, and lost. I really don't know what else to do.

She is sitting right next to me as I drive us home from her voice lesson in complete silence. We're only two feet apart, but it feels like we are on different planets.

I feel like I have exhausted all the resources available to me. I tried medicating her. I tried taking her to therapy. It helped her emotionally, but she is still failing in school, which I don't understand. She is so smart! Why can't she just be normal?

Abi is her name. She is my teenage daughter. She was diagnosed with attention deficit hyperactivity disorder (ADHD) when she was already in middle school. It was late for her to be diagnosed, and I don't know if that's good or bad, but that's what I am dealing with right now.

I tried getting her a coach who would help her get organized. She turned down tutors, saying that she did not need them, and the coach did not do much. Abi already knew everything the coach was trying to teach her. Well, she knew it in theory, but getting her to apply all those organizational skills in practice was like pulling teeth.

My mind keeps repeating the awful conversation we just had minutes ago.

"Abi, I just don't know what else to do," I said. "I feel like we have tried everything with you and nothing has changed. You are still failing most of your subjects at school. I feel desperate!"

"Well, that's your problem, not mine," she replied sharply.

That short phrase struck me like lightning, instantly paralyzing my ability to speak or even think. Ugh! It's a punch in the gut.

I can't believe she just said that to me. Does she understand how hurtful that sounds to me? Still shaken up and heavy-hearted, I drop her off at her grandma's house and head to a store—anywhere I can be alone with my thoughts.

* * *

It was at that moment I decided I needed help. So with this feeling of a mountain tied to my chest, I called the only person who seemed to know the answer to everything: my mentor, my life coach, Tamara. I told her about what happened, trying to sound lighter than I actually felt, but her answer surprised me: "Stop complaining. Everything is good with you. You are doing just fine, and so is your daughter. You just need to let her figure it out and lighten this tight grip you've got on her. It's suffocating her. And you."

I did not anticipate such an answer. I was expecting something like, "Try exorcism." (Just joking.) This answer seemed too simple. It seemed almost like cheating: *Worry less and let go, and let what you want come to you.*

And then it dawned on me: I had been trying to fix Abi this whole time—ever since she was diagnosed. But the truth was, Abi could not be fixed. She was not broken, and something that isn't broken doesn't need to be fixed.

She was just who she was. In fact, she might have been more in touch with who she was than most of us. Even when she was not comfortable with it, at least she knew who she was.

And who she was not.

When I (or anyone else) tried to make her fit into a standardized scenario that "should fit" kids her age, it just did not work.

* * *

I had always been a straight-A student myself. I finished high school a valedictorian. I graduated from the University of California, Davis, with the highest honors in both my bachelor's and master's degrees. I was a college professor, teaching biological and health sciences at a private school, so for me to have a child who was failing in school was completely devastating and unacceptable. I took it as a personal failure.

Little did I understand that my daughter, as much as I loved her, was not an extension of me. She had been her own person with her own path, life ambitions, and passions and wishes all along. Her ADHD only enabled her to be more unique without conforming to the standardized norms of today's society, school system, and behavioral standards—the standards I grew up with and accepted as "the right way."

Abi was like many other kids with ADHD, who comprise 5 percent of all kids between the ages of five and seventeen. Many go undiagnosed.

As the parent of an ADHD child, I know that I am not alone with my feelings. I have met many other moms and dads of ADHD kids who feel the same: our children do not fit the standard framework set by the school system and the society in which we (our generation) were raised. When we try to squeeze our ADHD kids into this standardized framework that is "supposed to fit," it does not work.

So what is the solution? That's what this book is all about. What I will discuss is how to create a new framework to fit the child, instead of the other way around. If the shoe does not fit, do not try to squeeze into it on anyway. Just change the shoe. Parents of ADHD kids must create a new framework that works for their individual child rather than for everyone else.

How it All Started

*We cannot change what we are not aware of, and once
we are aware, we cannot help but change.*
—Sheryl Sandberg

Let's rewind a couple of years.

My relationship with Abi was in the dumps. There was a lot of yelling, door-slamming, and arguing, followed by silence—long periods of silence, on both our sides. We weren't talking. That was the worst.

This was Abi at thirteen:

Before this, all through the elementary school, up through the fifth grade, Abi was an excellent student, getting mostly As and Bs. Yes, it took her a long time to get her homework done, but I did not put two and two together.

However, by the time she moved to middle school and into the sixth grade, she had started falling seriously behind. She also began showing signs of depression and anxiety, including frequent emotional meltdowns, crying easily whenever even slightly intimidated, not turning in assignments at school, and so on.

Being a bright girl, Abi figured out that it would be a good idea for her to see a therapist, and she asked for it. That's when we found a wonderful psychologist, Dr. Ruth, who spent a few sessions with Abi and then called Abi's dad and me and asked to see us.

Dr. Ruth sat us down and told us frankly what she thought: Abi could be suicidal.

What? I thought in disbelief. Yes, I knew about teen depression and teen suicide—in theory—but I never expected it to hit this close to home.

This was a wake-up call for us, and we were afraid that Abi could hurt herself.

Dr. Ruth was the first one who suggested that Abi's depression stemmed from attention deficit. I did not believe this diagnosis at first. Dr. Ruth recommended that we take Abi for a psychiatric evaluation to see if she indeed had ADHD. Soon after, we took Abi to a child psychiatrist for tests and diagnosis. After some testing and interviewing, with input from schoolteachers, Abi was diagnosed with Combined ADHD with anxiety and depression.

This was an eye-opener. I was in shock. But at the same time, the doctor's conclusion made ADHD more real to me—because frankly, up until this point, I did not believe that ADHD was a real thing. I thought it was a label slapped on lazy and unruly kids who were overdiagnosed and misdiagnosed half the time.

This realization devastated me at first. In fact, I wanted to scream, "Why can't I just have a normal child?!!!"

And then I went through the five stages of grief. You know: denial, anger, bargaining, depression, and acceptance. Sometimes I am still going through these stages. They come and go in waves, and every once in a while, they all hit at once.

After we got the diagnosis, we tried medicating Abi.

We first tried Concerta, which made Abi feel "foggy." Then we tried Vyvanse, which made her feel "like a robot." We tried Ritalin, Adderall— none of them stuck. They made Abi feel either sick or "not herself," which she did not like. Since the drugs did not work for Abi, she refused to take them, and I did not push.

Then we tried therapy.

Since Dr. Ruth was not a child psychologist, she recommended that we find a specialist in child and teen therapy with an emphasis on ADHD. We found a child psychologist, Sophia, who specialized in kids with ADHD, and for some time, I drove Abi to see Sophia week after week, month after month. It helped a bit; Abi received some emotional support from an adult with some tips and tricks on how to manage her ADHD.

We also tried tutors, coaches, and camps.

The main problem, though, was that I wanted to *fix* her—my daughter! But I couldn't, because my old way of thinking and trying to get Abi to

Gelena Gorelik

comply and conform to the established norms always led to the same old results.

The truth was, I could not fix Abi. Abi was just Abi.

The pivotal conversation came when she said straight to my face, "Well, that's your problem, not mine."

This was rock bottom and a wake-up call for me. My mentor and coach told me, "Lighten the grip; everything is actually fine." This made me reassess my standing with my daughter, my position, the way I was viewing her ADHD, and the way I was trying to fix her.

I realized that there were some things I was powerless to change in spite of my education, preparation, and experience. However, I could change the way I approached the situation. So I made a decision to look at Abi and her ADHD not as a problem but as an opportunity for *me* to grow—emotionally, intellectually, and spiritually.

* * *

I began to educate myself. I bought and read a ton of books, including *Your Defiant Teen* by Russell A. Barkley, *Smart but Scattered Teens* by Richard Guare, *From Chaos to Calm* by Janet E. Heininger and Sharon K. Weiss, and many others.

For me, Kathleen Nadeau's *Understanding Girls with ADHD* was the most influential and impactful. I began to have an idea of what my little girl was going through. Of course, I could not fully comprehend the complexity of her feelings and emotions in dealing with ADHD every day, every hour, but it gave me a different perspective and appreciation of her daily experience in school, in social life, and at home.

I then registered for and attended lots of seminars and webinars. I watched a multitude of educational videos and TED talks and even signed up for some courses. And an interesting thing started happening. As I learned more and more about ADHD, Abi started responding to me differently. She started warming up to me. Perhaps she finally felt that I was no longer trying to *fix* her but rather to *understand* her. Perhaps this made her feel less alone. She finally felt that she had someone at home who could understand—or at least accept—her just the way she was.

Little by little, I began seeing a change in our relationship. During Abi's junior year of high school, I took the kids on a spring-break trip to

Los Angeles. Abi took some of her friends, and her younger brother, Sam, took some of his. I rented a van, and we drove to Southern California for five days. The kids had a blast! They went together to Universal Studios and Six Flags Magic Mountain, played on the beach, and explored the cities of Los Angeles and Hollywood. This was probably the most exciting and memorable spring break they had in high school, and I felt fortunate for the opportunity to do this for them.

In this picture, Abi is the third from the right, and Sam is the first boy from the left.

Abi was smiling and laughing again, and chatting with me again. Our relationship was warming up and turning much more positive. In fact, I felt that I had gained a friend in her, and she had gained a friend in me as well.

Today, Abi, who recently graduated from high school, is doing better than ever. She is a bright young lady and a beautiful and confident college student who loves to sing and cook. Our relationship is flourishing and growing every day. I feel more connected with her than ever before, and our connection is growing stronger every year.

But it took a lot of work on my end, and time!

And patience!

Looking back on those years, I wish I'd had more help and support through this process. I think it got better because I realized that I was the one who needed to grow up. I was the one who needed to be educated and informed. I was the one who had to change. I learned much about ADHD in the process, but more importantly, I learned a great deal about myself and my daughter.

* * *

I believe that our children are our biggest teachers. They teach us love, patience, and acceptance—the most important human qualities that we experience in this world. I realized that I had to help other parents like me with ADHD kids so they did not have to go through the pain and isolation that I did.

I found some interesting statistics. Check these out:

- 5 percent of kids between the ages of five and seventeen are diagnosed with ADHD.
- Most of these kids have another mood disorder to accompany ADHD.
- Kids with ADHD are seven times more likely to commit suicide.
- *Parents* of kids with ADHD are ten times more likely to commit suicide.

This last one blew me away. It meant that we, the parents of ADHD kids, need all the help and support we can get. So I made it my mission to help other parents of ADHD kids.

I signed up to receive life-coach training from the Center for Strategic Intervention, which was founded by my teachers, Mark and Magali Peysha. They are the authors of *The Strategic Intervention Handbook* and leading educators in Strategic Intervention Life Coaching. They have certified more than twelve thousand life coaches worldwide in this methodology.

The strategies I learned there help me to work with individuals and families as a life coach. Some of the coaching strategies I learned there were based on previous teachings and principles of world-renowned life coaches Tony Robbins and Chloe Madanes. I became a certified coach and a practitioner of excellence and completed some additional training in advanced relationship coaching and advanced elite coach training courses.

In this book, I share with you all my knowledge and experience from coaching and teaching, my experience as a health care professional, and my experience as a mom so that you don't have to walk through the process of figuring it out alone.

This book is a complete A-to-Z blueprint that provides you with step-by-step instructions for achieving peace at home and the harmony in your relationship with your spirited child that you crave and deserve. Here you will find specific tools and instructions, right down to what to say and do in situations to stop conflict and build a fantastic relationship with your child.

As you read the book, the following will happen:

- You will gain a fresh perspective on ADHD. (Hint: it has its advantages too!)
- You will understand the needs of your child/teen and how those needs are being met or not met.
- You will realize that you are the leader who must practice effective communication and discover what makes a good leader and why you need to be one.
- You will learn why you must reframe your focus today to transform your relationship with your child/teen.

One word of caution: if you are looking for a magic bullet, a quick fix, or an "easy" button (like in that *Staples* commercial), and you just want to fix your kid with a Band-Aid-like solution, this book probably won't work for you.

Also, this book is not just some parenting advice. I won't tell you how to raise your child (only you know what's best for your kid). The goal here is a systemic, fundamental, and profound shift in your perspective and overall well-being and livelihood.

I have written this book exclusively for parents of ADHD kids and teens to show you that you can restore peace at home and rebuild your relationship with your child in just five steps. I will dedicate a chapter to each step, with specific strategies and assignments you can practice and implement immediately. Here they are:

- **Step 1: Reframe the Situation.** Stop seeing ADHD as a disorder and start seeing it as something that makes our kids stand out—something that makes them special and unique.

- **Step 2: Understand Your Child's Needs.** See how your child's critical needs for well-being are met or not met and what you can do to get those needs met so your child won't have to look elsewhere to meet them in unhealthy ways.

- **Step 3: Meet *Your* Needs.** This one is overlooked by a lot of parents. We (especially moms) feel guilty focusing on our needs, but when our needs are not met, we cannot be the best that we can be for our children. This step is essential.

- **Step 4: Learn to Respond, Not React.** There is a big difference between the two, and you must know it and apply it. We will discuss what effective responding is, and I will give you very specific *to do* and *to say* tips for effective communication to transform your relationships instantly.

- **Step 5: Become a Leader, Not a Manager.** Learn what it means to be the leader of your household and why you must become one today. We often get sidetracked and stuck in managing things and putting out fires after the disasters have already happened. Instead, I will show you how to stay ahead of the game and inspire others to be the best they can be.

Now I am going to ask you to stop for a moment and think of your last interaction with your spirited child … and the interaction before that … and the one before that. Take a deep breath and, for a few moments, imagine what your life would look like if your child got up on time, went to bed when told, got homework done every day, kept a neat bedroom, completed household chores, and acted polite and considerate.

Ah! Wouldn't that be nice!

If you really think about this, what you are really after is peace and harmony at home and in your relationship with your kid. What I described in the paragraph above is just a positive side effect—an outcome of having a good relationship with your child.

Yes, it will take some work and determination from you, but I know you have it in you. With that, let's proceed to step 1.

Step 1
Reframe the Situation

Everybody is a genius. But if you judge a fish by its ability to climb a tree it will live its whole life believing that it's stupid.
—Unknown

In this chapter, we will reframe and redefine ADHD and attention deficit disorder (ADD). We're going to move away from looking at ADD/ADHD as a disorder and start really looking at it as a different way of processing information. Here is a quick snapshot of what we're going to cover:

- **First**, I'm going to explain the difference between spirited kids and compliant kids and how they are different from the inside in terms of the physiology of the ADD/ADHD brain.
- **Next**, I'm going to talk about why they are the way they are and how they are actually wired for survival. I'm going to discuss brain chemistry and how the ADHD brain is different from the ordinary brain. Now, please note, I didn't say *normal* brain; I said *ordinary*, because I don't want you to think of ADHD as something that's abnormal.
- **Finally**, I'm going to show you how to respond to different behaviors, specifically difficult and aggressive behavior; explain why teenage kids and preteens are actually more aggressive than adults and younger children; and let you know what you can do about it starting today.

ADHD Brain Anatomy and Physiology

I would like to start with a mini-quiz—a little question for you. What do you think these people have in common: Will Smith, Albert Einstein, Whoopi Goldberg, John F. Kennedy, Jim Carey, and Leonardo Da Vinci?

If you said that they have ADHD or are believed to have had ADHD, you are correct. Other famous people who have or are believed to have had ADHD include:

- Albert Einstein
- the Wright Brothers
- Isaac Newton
- Henry Ford
- Alexander Fleming
- Galileo
- Mark Twain
- Agatha Christie
- Thomas Edison
- Vincent van Gogh
- Emma Watson
- Robin Williams
- Elvis Presley
- Michael Jordan
- Steve Jobs
- Mozart

The list goes on and on.

Just look at those names and think about how brilliant all these people are or were. They all had these special brains.

Now, a bit of science. If you looked at a brain scan that visually reflects the brain's metabolic rate and compared side-by-side the scans of an ADHD brain and an ordinary brain, you would notice that the ADHD brain looks less active than the regular one.

Does that surprise you? Would you expect the ADHD brain to look more "hyper" than the ordinary brain? Why does the ADHD brain appear to have a slower metabolism and lower activity?

Let's take a look and find out, using the following illustration, what is going on in the brain and why an ADHD brain scan would appear less active than an ordinary one by discussing a little anatomy and physiology. I promise to keep this very simple. Take a close look at this picture:

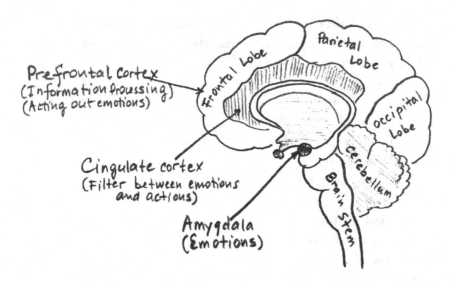

In this picture, I have indicated the important functions of the parts I want to point out: the *amygdala*, responsible for emotions; the *prefrontal cortex*, responsible for information processing and acting out those emotions; and the *cingulate cortex*, which serves as the filter between the two.

When your amygdala gets activated, you feel certain emotions, but it depends on the situation as to whether you act on them. If your higher brain (prefrontal cortex) decides that it's okay to act, you might do just that.

For example, when you feel happy and something makes you smile, you will smile or laugh if you consider that behavior appropriate in a given situation. However, if you are at a meeting and you glance at your phone and see a funny message, you won't start laughing, because it would be inappropriate under the circumstances. Your prefrontal cortex makes a decision as to whether acting out this emotion is okay or not okay.

Let's say you're watching the news, and you learn about a horrible disaster that happened on the opposite end of the world from you. You would probably get less upset about it than if such a disaster happened close to your home. You process the information and make a choice of which emotional responses to act on.

Perhaps you feel emotionally triggered about something at work. Let's say you are talking to a customer, and you cannot really show that you're feeling angry or frustrated. Your prefrontal cortex will not allow you to act out that frustration if you don't want to lose this customer.

(A quick side note: As people get older, their prefrontal cortex sometimes starts to deteriorate, and their emotional responses are no longer properly controlled. This is why, at times, elderly folks tend to get emotional over the smallest things—the emotional amygdala wins over the logical prefrontal cortex.)

When information travels from the amygdala to the prefrontal cortex, it travels through a structure called the cingulate cortex. The cingulate cortex works like a filter or brake between your emotions and your actions, giving your prefrontal cortex time to process and sort whether acting out an emotion is appropriate. Returning to the situation when you are feeling upset or angry with a customer who's being especially annoying, your cingulate cortex allows reaction time between the amygdala and prefrontal cortex. This keeps you from expressing your anger or frustration to your customer.

That's how nerve impulses typically travel—from the amygdala through the cingulate cortex to the prefrontal cortex, and then you either act on the emotion generated in the amygdala or you don't.

In the ADHD brain, this filter—the cingulate cortex—works more slowly than in an ordinary brain. It's not keeping up with the amygdala's activity.

Think of the cingulate cortex as the brakes on your acting out. The cingulate cortex in the ADHD brain lags behind. It's not as active. The brakes are not working as well. As a result, in the ADHD brain, the prefrontal cortex ends up acting out emotions without proper control.

This is why people with ADHD tend to act out emotionally—the filter is not keeping up with the nerve impulses firing from the amygdala. This is what it feels like to your child. Feelings and thoughts are firing super-fast, and the filter between emotion and expression cannot keep up.

Just imagine what it would feel like if your brain went a million miles a minute, jumping from one thought to the next, to the next, to the next, because the brakes that would cause you to stay with one particular thought don't work very well.

On one hand, this is what allows people with ADHD to think so fast; on the other, it leaves them unable to concentrate on stuff that cannot keep them interested, like a boring article or a dull chapter out of a geography textbook, or writing an essay on a topic for which they have no feeling or interest.

Teenage Brain Anatomy and Physiology

Now I want to talk a little more about a teenage brain specifically. If your kids are not teens yet, just hang on, because it's coming. Get prepared and get this information under your belt, because this is important.

Science shows that teenage brains are wired for survival. We all know that teenagers tend to be more aggressive than younger kids or adults. But why? I want you to understand where that's coming from. Evolution is to blame.

Aggression is the evolutionary tool for establishing identity and power in a community or tribe. Thousands of years ago, during the Stone Age, individuals who were more aggressive were the ones who survived and led their tribes to survival. We (you and me and our kids) are their descendants.

Thousands (or even only hundreds) of years ago, by the time you reached puberty, you were considered an adult member of your tribe or community. Think of old tribal ceremonies welcoming thirteen-year-old boys into manhood. Even today in Judaism and other religions, this coming-of-age ceremony takes place for boys around their thirteenth birthday, when they are considered to become men. Historically, puberty has been the time for teenagers to establish themselves socially. Back in those days, how would you establish yourself socially?

Think about that.

You would do it by being more aggressive (and, perhaps, more violent) than your peers. It was the more aggressive individuals who got to become leaders of the tribe. They were the alpha males and females. This is genetically imprinted in all of us, and that's important to keep in mind when we talk to our preteens and teens.

Consider this as a normal part of human evolution. It's just part of becoming an adult. It will pass as the brain matures—which, as many know, happens by the age of twenty-five years, not earlier. Yes, we have evolved as a society, but our brain chemistry cannot keep up with how fast our society is changing and evolving. Our brains are still ancient.

In fact, our brain physiology is the same as it was thousands of years ago. You can start understanding why teens and preteens behave this way because you know now that evolution is to blame. However, let's focus on what we can do today, as parents of our amazing ADHD kids and teens, to help them establish themselves in a good way and for us to have a good relationship with them in the process.

To learn more, please check out the "Sibling Rivalry" bonus chapter and "Parent's Resource Guide to ADHD Dos and Don'ts" in the appendix of this book.

Where Is Your Focus?

I want you to shift your focus to what actually matters the most. The most important thing here is your happy and healthy child. Period. That's what we, as parents, *really* want for our children. Everything else is secondary. So shift your focus to what is really important.

Now think, just think: what horrible things will happen if your child does not go to college or finish high school, or make her bed in the morning, or clean up his room? I mean, how terrible would that be? Honestly, these thoughts used to upset me.

However, just compare these to the problems of parents whose kids are gravely ill, have serious mental or physical abnormalities, or worse, are missing. Next to those problems, your kid is actually doing pretty well, wouldn't you agree? It's all a matter of perspective.

There was an old joke (which you might know) of a girl writing to her parents from college saying that she got pregnant, got infected with HIV, is dropping out of school, and a whole bunch of other things that would scare and devastate her parents. Then she finished her letter with, "I am just kidding. I failed one course. I am really sorry." Imagine the relief of her parents at the end.

Again, it's all a matter of perspective. Shift your focus to what really matters.

ADHD Is Neurodiversity, Not a Disability

Take a look at this picture. What do you see?

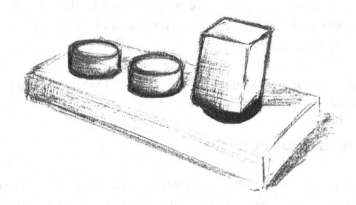

A square peg does not fit into a round hole, right?

The two round pegs you see are like other (non-ADHD) kids, or us and our parents, fitting into the frames set by previous generations, teachers, trainers, mentors, etc. Our ADHD kids are like the square pegs that cannot possibly fit into the old frames of the round holes where we, and others like us, used to fit in.

Sometimes we're working from old frames set up by previous generations. These frames may represent how our parents raised us and how our teachers trained us. Unfortunately, these old frames no longer work—not the way they used to, anyway. Times and rules are changing quickly as our society and technology evolve faster than ever.

Your child has been born into this new time with new rules. The set of rules you were born into no longer applies to your kids, whether they have ADHD or not—and even more so for the ADHD kids and kids with special needs and learning disabilities. It's like having your kids play with your childhood toys and expecting them to enjoy that. It's just not going to happen, because your children have been born into a different time, a different generation, with different tools and toys and different expectations.

You need to shift your expectations; they cannot be the same as the ones your parents had of you. Your expectations of your child need to evolve with the new framework of the current generation, especially when it comes to kids with ADHD and other types of neurodiversity.

For one thing, stop thinking of ADHD as some sort of disability. Start thinking of it as a variety, not a disorder. Yes, we know that ADHD stands for attention deficit hyperactivity *disorder*, and *disorder* means to most of us "out of order." But we must stop labeling our kids that way. ADHD is just a variety of how they are wired for survival. Stop thinking of this as a disorder and start treating it as diversity.

There are, believe it or not, certain advantages to ADHD. For one, the ADHD brain works faster than everybody else's. In the Stone Age, people with ADHD (note that they were not labeled as such back then) were actually considered extremely valuable to their tribes and communities. These folks were great at hunting and gathering because they could think and respond faster than others.

Advantages of ADHD

- brain works faster than everyone else's
- great at hunting and gathering
- excellent at brainstorming
- able to think outside the box
- resilient
- able to hyperfocus
- comfortable outside the comfort zone

Today, people with ADHD are great at brainstorming and creativity. They are artistic; they think outside the box. They process information differently than everybody else. And they're very resilient. Why resilient? If you think about it, ADHD people move on to the next thought that occurs to them so quickly that they don't dwell on the negative. That actually oftentimes makes them tougher and stronger than others.

People with ADHD are very comfortable going outside of a comfort zone and thinking beyond the "normal" and "regular." When they're passionate about something, they can hyperfocus, which allows them to become extremely successful in their area of interest.

Gelena Gorelik

Thinking Outside the Box

Let's talk some more on the subject of thinking outside the box. In fact, some say people with ADHD "don't even know where the box is."

I want to give you a small example using my daughter Abi. When she was in fifth grade, the teacher gave the class a little art assignment. The teacher had the kids take their shoe, trace the contour of the shoe on a piece of paper, and then color it with patterns and colors to represent their personality.

What did Abi do? Of all the kids, she was the only one who took her shoe and drew it sideways, so it didn't look like a step—it actually looked like a shoe from a side view. Then she colored it to reflect her personality.

I thought it ended up looking pretty cool—not like everyone else's. It was a really unique way of approaching this project. The teacher, however, didn't see it that way. She considered Abi disobedient for not following instructions. Needless to say, the teacher marked Abi's work down and made her redo the project to be like everyone else's.

I was saddened and disappointed by this response from the teacher. For Abi, this was quite upsetting—she was being punished for being creative, for being an individual, which must have been devastating for her.

On a grand scale, this is typical of how individuality and creativity is beaten out of our kids by the school system, the community, the older generations, and so on. This is a sad reflection of how our society works. We're trying to squeeze kids who are creative, gifted, and talented into a standardized-thinking box. The truth is, they don't fit into that standard box; in fact, they resist it and hate it. Yet we still try to make them fit into something that does not fit—like trying to squeeze into shoes that are two sizes too small.

It hurts. It's uncomfortable. It's unnecessary.

The way you approach your child, the way you raise your child, should fit the child, not the average approach to an average student. ADHD kids are amazing, unique, and creative. Don't ever let your child or yourself believe otherwise.

> **COACHING TIP**
>
> I want you to start thinking of your ADHD kid as an amazing person. How is your child special? What are your child's talents? Write them all out. Come up with a list of at least ten things that make your child amazing, and then place that list somewhere where your child can see it. Watch what happens in the days that follow.

ADHD and Enterpreneurship

Interestingly, I have recently read in *Entrepreneur* magazine that a lot of successful entrepreneurs have ADHD. In fact, it is the ADHD that helps them become successful. To become a prosperous entrepreneur, one needs to have a unique way of thinking and an ability to hyper focus. One must have a unique approach to problem-solving, nonstandard ways of brainstorming, and an ability to think quickly—and that's exactly what ADHD people have.

In fact, I know someone personally who made it to the *Forbes* "Top 30 Under 30" thanks to ADHD and a nonstandard way of thinking and problem-solving. This individual had a rocky start and struggled through school but ended up becoming very successful professionally, financially, and personally.

So let's celebrate these wonderful, positive qualities of ADHD. People with ADD/ADHD have high social intelligence. They have great empathy for others. They have exceptional abilities, and they're very talented—sometimes in music, art, sports, or business.

The bottom line is that ADHD people can rock our world and make a difference if we let them and embrace them just the way they are. Look up Michael Jordan's story on the internet to learn how ADHD allowed him to hyperfocus and become the basketball legend he is today.

Difficult and Aggressive Behavior

Let's talk about dealing with difficult or aggressive behavior, especially because in the teenage years, it's more prominent. If your kids are not teenagers yet, pay attention, because it's coming. Be prepared and get armed with this useful information.

I want start with the idea that we all are spiritual beings having a physical experience in this world. Stephen Covey, author of *The 7 Habits of Highly Effective People*, said, "We are not human beings on a spiritual journey. We are spiritual beings on a human journey."

We all come into this world with the same common plan: to create our own reality. Who is that creator inside each and every one of us? It's the extension of source energy, the inner being. Some call it consciousness; some call it the soul or spirit or intuition. Whatever you are comfortable calling it, this is the core of who you really are.

For the purposes of this book, I will use the term *Inner Being*.

We feel happiest and freest when we are in agreement with our Inner Being. And we are happiest when we create, because that's what the Inner Being wants: *to create*. The opposite is also true. When we feel that our power of control and ability to create our own reality are taken away from us, we feel unhappy, unfree. We feel loss, and for most of us, loss feels painful.

Our children came into this world to create, just like us. They are here to create their own reality, their own world—to manifest their dreams, wishes, and desires. So when the power of control, the power to create their reality, is taken away from them, they feel loss. Even if there's nothing taken away from them materially or physically, they still feel the loss.

Keep in mind, the loss of expectation is just as tangible and painful as the loss of a physical object. For example, a man was working for five years at the same company, same position, waiting to get promoted. The man was confident that he would get promoted as soon as an opportunity presented itself in the company. However, when the opportunity for a promotion came, the position was given to someone else. The man was upset, hurt, and felt powerless and angry. Even though he did not really lose anything, he lost the expectation, which was just as painful as losing something real.

> ## Consider Their Point of View
>
> Our children come into this world to create their own reality. When their power to control their own reality is taken away, they feel loss.

I was at a department store the other day and witnessed a very unpleasant scene. A two-year-old threw herself on the floor in a full-blown temper tantrum, complete with yelling, kicking, and screaming. I don't know what the demand was, but obviously the little girl expected her mom to buy her something (probably some toy or a treat) and the mom refused. The unmet expectation was painful enough that the toddler threw this awful tantrum. Maybe she knew she could get away with it, maybe not, but this episode was a perfect example of how we respond to unmet expectations.

In older kids, teenagers, and adults, tantrums may not manifest in throwing oneself on the floor, kicking and screaming; they may take different forms. But the bottom line is the same: when there's a loss of expectation, we feel emotional pain, and that pain needs a release. It feels the same way to you as well. When your expectation and your reality do not match, you feel unhappy, as this mismatch causes emotional pain.

Emotional pain is felt and experienced by the brain exactly same way as any physical pain. To the brain, pain, whether emotional or physical, is perceived the same. Just think of how powerless and painful it feels when, for example, your boss is being unfair to you, or when you're stuck in traffic and you are already late for a meeting. If you feel there's nothing you can do to control the situation, you feel powerless, which feels really painful.

When we're feeling emotional pain, it normally wants to release itself in the form of anger. So pain leads to anger. However, anger takes a lot of energy, which is not sustainable in the long run. We cannot stay at that level of energy to continue feeling angry, and if the situation is prolonged, the anger turns to sadness, a lower-energy state.

To summarize, loss of expectation or feeling powerless in trying to create one's own experience leads to pain, which leads to anger, which if it continues for a while, turns to sadness and depression. This is why depression is so prevalent among ADHD kids, especially among teenagers. It's because sometimes they feel so powerless that their powerlessness leads to feeling angry, which leads to depression.

> ### Understand
>
> *Loss* of expectation leads to *pain.*
>
> *Pain* leads to *anger* (or sadness).
>
> We feel *angry* when we feel *powerless.*

Tony Robbins came up with the term *crazy eight* to explain how most of us, when we are upset, turn to anger, followed by sadness, then back to anger, and then to sadness, and on and on.

Angry <–> Sad

Is this crazy eight doomed to go on forever? Of course not. Here is what you can do to get out of this cycle for yourself and for your child or teen.

What You Can Do Today

The crazy eight will stop for you when you choose to step out of it by reframing the situation. When your reality does not match your expectations, you feel unhappy. So the first step is to stop and think, *How can my reality and expectations match up?*

Usually, to make this happen, you need to change your reality (which is not always easy), change your expectations, or change your framework. We have talked about trying to fit a square peg into a round hole; the reality does not fit the expectation, and you cannot change your square peg. So you must change the hole—in other words, reframe the situation.

In this next part, I will walk you through four things you can do right now, starting today, whenever your child behaves in a difficult or aggressive manner.

1. Question Your Motivation

You must ask yourself the following:

- What does my child's aggression or anger make me feel? Does it make me feel aggression too? Do I feel aggressive in response to my child's aggression?
- When my child is acting out in anger, does that make me angry, too? Does it make me feel like I have to control my child? (This is very common, because you too are trying to control your reality; therefore, most likely, you will want to control your child so that you can control your reality.)
- What emotion happens in me when my child is aggressive? What does my child's aggression or anger evoke in me?

2. Recognize Your Response

The next step is to recognize that your child's aggression sometimes summons the aggression in you. We can blame the mirror neurons for that, actually. Mirror neurons are the nerve cells in your brain that make you yawn when you see someone else yawning and make you laugh when you see someone laughing uncontrollably.

I can personally admit that when my child was angry, and I observed her being angry, it used to make me angry as well. This was a conditional response, which means that my feelings depended on my child's behavior.

When your child is behaving well, your expectations and your reality match, and you feel at ease. It feels good because at that moment, you are aligned internally. When your child is angry or aggressive, your expectations and reality do not match (just like they don't match for your child in that moment), and you feel misaligned internally. When we are not aligned internally, we are not thriving. What does that mean?

Going back to the notion that we are spiritual beings having a human experience, we must accept that each of us is an extension of source energy.

Gelena Gorelik

I refer to this as the Inner Being—the very core of each one of us, our consciousness that creates our reality.

When your ego and your Inner Being are not in agreement, not in alignment, you feel uneasy. In other words, when your mind and your heart are not in agreement, you feel unhappy or discontent from yourself. You cannot thrive when there is no inner alignment. Therefore, your alignment with your Inner Being is very important.

We will talk more about inner alignment in the upcoming chapters (step 2 and step 3), including what it is, how important it is, and how to get it.

3. Realize Your Power

Realize that your Inner Being the core of who you really are, the extension of source energy that you are, does not want to be aggressive in return. Your Inner Being wants to actually love your child. You want to focus on your Inner Being and practice saying to your child, "I know you feel angry, and I love you anyway."

Just practice saying "I love you anyway," and then really focus on that loving feeling. Do not focus on your child's anger. Do not focus on your own anger. Focus on loving.

You want to move away from your feelings being dependent on your child's behavior. How your child behaves should not affect how you feel emotionally. I know that very often, we do feel dependent on how others feel and behave, but that is exactly what we need to work on. All of us need to work on that.

Whatever your child is doing or not doing is irrelevant. I know this statement may seem shocking at first, but just bear with me, and as you keep going through the chapters in this book, it will make more and more sense to you.

What's important is the misalignment of you with your Inner Being, which actually feels painful to you.

When we feel misaligned, we feel bad, and for that we often blame someone else (in this case, our kids). However, the truth is, the only thing you can truly control is the alignment between you and you. What really matters is your alignment between your mind and your heart, or between your ego and your Inner Being, or between your mind and your spirit or soul.

What your child is doing (or not doing) is irrelevant. What is important is the misalignment of you with your Inner Being, which feels bad to you. You may be blaming it on your child, but the truth is, the only thing you can really control is the alignment between you and you.

Our children's aggression is their response to us feeling that they need to be different or act different in order for us to feel better, and they will *not* let us have that. We must love *unconditionally*.

When you want your child to act differently so you can feel better, you are practicing conditional love, conditional life, and conditional being.

When your mind and your spirit are aligned, when they're on the same page, that's when you feel good. Since what your Inner Being really wants is to love, when you are in alignment with that part of yourself, it won't matter how your child behaves.

It's your mind or your ego that says, "My child is behaving in a way she shouldn't." But where that *should* and *shouldn't* come from is the conditions that were programmed into you by your parents, your teachers, previous generations, and your schools.

When Abi drew her shoe sideways for that school assignment, she did not perform according to the teacher's expectation (condition). If the teacher appreciated the product of Abi's creativity rather than her ability to satisfy preset conditions, both Abi and her teacher would have benefited from that, and their relationship would have benefited from it too. However, because the teacher put her condition first, the whole experience was frustrating for both of them.

If you put conditions like completing household chores, getting good grades, doing as told, or acting "normal" first, you are living a conditional life and demonstrating conditional love to your child. Your child's difficult and aggressive behavior is actually a response to your feeling that your child needs to be different or act different in order for you to feel better.

ADHD kids simply will not let you have that because that would be a conditional life and conditional love.

Instead, love your child unconditionally. When you want your child to act differently so you can feel better, that is practicing conditional love, conditional life, and conditional being. It is your job and responsibility to find alignment with yourself—alignment with your Inner Being.

You might ask: "How will this approach help prepare my child for the 'real world' and raise kids to be functional adults?" I want to ask you to be patient with the process here and remind you that it is really all about prioritizing the health and well-being of your child and you, because in the long run, nothing else matters if you don't have that.

Bear with me, as I have gone through this myself with my daughter. I have faced the same fears and challenges, and I can tell you honestly that this approach actually better prepares ADHD children to be functional adults than trying to squeeze them into frameworks that don't work for them.

I personally had to fight back a lot of naysayers, including my own parents, Abi's dad, and even her younger brother. You might have to do that, too. You must become your child's advocate at school and at home. As a result, you will have a much healthier, happier, stronger, and more confident child or teen—and a much healthier and more harmonious relationship between you and your child. ADHD children will actually grow up as more-functional adults with this approach than if they constantly feel inadequate because they cannot satisfy their parents' (or others') conditions and expectations.

When others easily cooperate or readily change their behavior so that we can feel better (like, in my case, my compliant child, Abi's brother), they're not really helping us grow because they're not forcing us to align with our Inner Being.

Our challenging spirited children are actually forcing us to focus on our alignment with who we really are. Think of it as a gift and an opportunity. This is a chance for us to discover the true power of self-alignment. In this sense, your child is actually being your teacher. How amazing is that!

4. Take the Path of Least Resistance

Believe it or not, this is what everything in nature does. Let some water flow down a rock, and it will find the path of least resistance. Electric current runs down the wire with the least resistance. When you take a boat, it's much easier to go downstream than up. For you, taking the path of least resistance means lightening the grip.

Your child is proving to you that you can't really be in charge forever. The more you try to control your child, the more your child will show you that you cannot and will not, the more resistance your child will put up, and the more your relationship with your child will suffer.

The path of least resistance for you is to self-talk into alignment. You need to practice this day after day, and gradually you will see the difference in the way your child responds to you. When you look at what your child is doing and don't like it, you can still look at your child with love and kindness because you are in alignment with yourself. Only from that place can you interact with your child successfully. When you are aligned on the inside—aligned with yourself—your relationship with yourself is in thriving mode. Once you are aligned and thriving, only then will your relationship with your child start thriving too.

> ### Just Remember
>
> If you interact with your child when you are frustrated, angry, or disappointed, you feel those emotions, because you are not in alignment with yourself. When you are not in alignment, you know it, because you feel bad emotionally.
>
> When you *are* in alignment, you feel good emotionally. You feel love, kindness, joy, curiosity, creativity, and inspiration. It's all about alignment!

If you feel judged by other people and their expectations when they say, for example, "What are you doing to discipline your child?" you could reply, "Well, I am loving him."

They might say, "Well, what are you going to do about this behavior or that behavior? Why is her room messy? Why are her grades so low?" To that you could reply, "Well, I'm just going to love her."

If they insist, "Well, you have to do something. You can't just go on and love your child," you can respond, "Yes I can, and I'm going to love my child until a perfect inspiration occurs to me. And so I'm going to love my child, and I'm going to love you, too, even though you're not in alignment with yourself either right now."

You see, the common problem is that you're trying to serve too many masters. You're trying to please too many people. You're trying to please your child, your spouse, your parents, schoolteachers, friends. You're trying to do right by all of them.

But guess what? There are too many people to please, and while you're trying to please them, you are ignoring the most important person: *you*, your Inner Being. Just say this: "When I am in alignment with my inner being and I am in thriving mode, I am open to the inspiration and receiving information from the universe, so I can say the right things at the right time, and I will be an influence for wonderful things to come to my child."

In the words of the teachings of Abraham-Hicks: "Talk to your children as much as you can, but never unless you are in a *very good mood*." Being in a very good mood means being in alignment—and knowing you're in alignment because you feel good emotionally. Only then can your children feel your unconditional love. Only from that place can you practice effective parenting.

I would like to wrap up this chapter with a quote from Russel Barkley: "Remember, the kids who need the most love will ask for it in the most unloving ways." Focus on your inner alignment and keep loving your kids unconditionally, regardless of how they behave.

Key Points

- Take your focus away from your child's ADHD or what your child cannot do. Instead, focus on the ultimate goal, which is a happy and healthy child.
- Remember that good grades and a clean room are only the means to this end goal. Shift your thinking from what is not working to

appreciating kids for the wonderful, creative, innovative thinkers that they are.

- Pay attention to your own inner alignment first; everything else will fall into place naturally.

Step 2
Understand Your Child's Needs

Allow children to be happy in their own way,
for what better way will they find?
—*Samuel Johnson*

In this chapter, we are moving on to step 2 of the five steps to restore peace at home and rebuild your relationship with your ADHD child or teen. We're going to focus on understanding your child's needs and what it means to really listen and understand what those needs are.

In this chapter, we will discuss the six human needs as defined by Tony Robbins. Here is a quick snapshot of what we're going to cover:

- **First**, I'm going to talk about which of those six needs are going to take the most attention in teenagers and children with ADHD.
- **Then**, I'm going to explain what happens when those needs are not met.
- **Finally**, I will suggest what you can do today to help meet your child's needs.

The Six Human Needs

Those of you who are familiar with the basics of psychology or have studied some health care fields are probably familiar with Maslow's hierarchy of needs, which is founded on the concept that the basic physiological needs (such as shelter, air, food, and water) must be met before the higher physiological and psychological needs (love, esteem, and self-actualization) are met. But that would be an entirely separate topic.

In this book, I will discuss the six human needs as defined by Tony Robbins. According to Robbins, pretty much everything we do, we do either to get pleasure or to avoid pain. These are our immediate and strongest motivators. For example, your child may do the dishes to please you and feel good about the completed task (pleasure) or to avoid getting yelled at (pain). Or you may go to work because you really love what you do and it gives you satisfaction and fulfillment (pleasure) or because you don't want to get fired (pain).

While pain and pleasure are our immediate motivators, in the grand scheme of things, we want to make sure that our six needs are met. The six human needs, as defined by Tony Robbins, are as follows:

1. ertainty
2. Variety
3. Love and connection
4. Significance
5. Growth
6. Contribution

When our needs are not met, we feel unfulfilled, unhappy, and misaligned; in other words, we are stressed in one way or another.

The Need for Certainty

This first need is by far the most fundamental of them all. If you were to compare this to Maslow's hierarchy of needs, this would be the basic foundational and physiological need, like safety, when your life is not in danger. Certainty includes having air, food, water, shelter, and security. It's the structure and stability we all need in our lives. If the need for certainty is not met, other needs matter less, because this is the first and most important one that must be met.

For kids, this need is absolutely vital. This is why, as we know, kids thrive on routine. Lack of certainty becomes an issue if, for example, money is a problem in the family, or there is a lot of yelling and arguing, or worse, there is physical abuse at home or school. Another example is if a family has to relocate frequently; in this situation, kids don't feel that certainty. If kids have to change schools once a year or more, or if their parents are going through a divorce, the kids are not certain where they will live. Another example is when children going home from school are not certain if they will get yelled at or punished when they get there.

The basics of certainty are food on the table, roof over the head, and some stability, structure, and certainty in knowing what is coming in the next hour, month, or year. The need for certainty is absolutely essential, and it is the number-one need that must be addressed. There are instances, however, when this need is met in unhealthy ways. Being stuck in a situation just because it feels familiar, even if the situation is painful, is not a healthy way to meet this need. This is why sometimes people stay in abusive relationships or hold on to physical or emotional pain; the situation is familiar and predictable. This is why some people are afraid to change jobs or move to another house—to take any sort of risk.

Remember the main character in *Eat, Pray, Love*? Toward the end of the story, she was afraid to fall in love because she was afraid to lose her balance—afraid to lose that certainty. However, she learned that sometimes "losing balance for love is a part of living a balanced life." This brings us to the second human need.

The Need for Variety

Ironically, the second most important need is the opposite of certainty— the need to have some uncertainty! In other words, we have a need for variety. If things are too stable and predictable, life can become stale and boring. We get uneasy when life is too predictable, so we need to change things up every so often.

There are healthy and unhealthy ways to meet this need. Healthy ways include going on vacation, traveling, reading a new book or story, going to see a movie, going to the theater, going to museums, or engaging in anything new and interesting. When you are doing those things, even for a couple of hours, you can escape into a different world or pretend reality.

Other ways to meet the need for variety could be trying a new food at a different restaurant, taking a new route when you are going home or going to school, or going anywhere. Learning a new song or dance or different routine, changing up the usual routine, meeting new people, changing jobs (for an adult), taking a new class—all are examples of healthy and constructive ways to fulfill the need for variety.

Unfortunately, there are also unhealthy and destructive ways people meet this need. Examples include experimenting with drugs, gambling, or becoming involved in criminal activities, such as stealing. For kids, meeting the need for variety in unhealthy ways can include skipping classes. For adults, it may be having an affair.

These are examples of destructive ways of meeting the Need for Variety. We want to make sure that when we feel uneasy or stuck, when we feel like things are getting stale and boring, that we find *healthy* ways to meet the need for variety.

The Need for Love and Connection

We must feel like we belong with someone. This is why we hang out with our friends. This is why people get married. This is why we have children. This is why even the most introverted introvert has friends and wants to be with a significant other, even for a little while.

I consider myself quite introverted, and one time I went on vacation by myself. I didn't have my kids with me. I didn't have my husband. I was just by myself. I went to Mexico to spend a week during winter break. This was my first time going anywhere by myself, and for the first three days, I loved it! I really enjoyed my solitude. I was reading my book; I was watching my movies that I wanted to see in the evenings; I was swimming in the pool; I was just doing all the things by myself.

But by day four, I started to feel like, "Hmm, something is missing. I need something." I realized that the "something" was connection. I needed to connect with others. So I went out and started talking to people and had a great time.

We crave that human connection. We need it. As much as we love our pets, we don't get the same need for love and connection fulfillment as we do with other human beings.

There are also unhealthy and destructive ways to meet this need. For example, if a woman sacrifices her own safety and subjects herself to an abusive relationship just to feel connected to someone, she is trying to meet the need for love and connection in an unhealthy way. For teenagers, it could be sexting or engaging in unprotected sex too soon or too early for their age. Some kids (and adults) get into this doormat-behavior attitude just so they can be connected with their peers, even if it means sacrificing their own interests.

This is why high school kids form clicks and groups. This is why kids can fall victim to bullying or cyberbullying (more on that later). The need for love and connection is profound.

The Need for Significance

The fourth need is the opposite of the third need. It's the need to stand out, to be separate from the crowd, or to feel special and important in one way or another. This is why we take selfies and put our pictures on social media. We need to feel special and let others know that our lives are interesting—that we are special.

Yes, we crave connection immensely, but at the same time, we need to separate and stand out. We long to be noticed by others, and we want to be admired and looked up to. This is why we dress up. This is why we put on makeup and jewelry and do our hair. This is why we post stuff on Facebook and Instagram—we want others to notice and like what we do. And the more "likes" we get on those social media posts, the better we feel.

This is why some people pursue higher degrees and build careers and climb that corporate ladder. This is why kids want to get As in school and get on the honor roll. These are some examples of healthy ways to get the need for significance met.

Unfortunately, as with the other needs we have discussed, there are unhealthy ways to meet this need. For example, bullying behavior is a way for bullies to get noticed and respected by others, even if it gets them in trouble. Bullies feels important and significant to their victims. Unfortunately, a lot of criminal activities, like the illegal use of guns, have become so common.

Gun violence, sexual violence, or any other violent behavior is a typical way of trying to meet that need of feeling power and control over another person—in other words, significance. Even using common passive-aggressive behavior just to make oneself feel important and to get noticed is an unhealthy way to meet the need for significance. When the need for significance is not met, or is met in a destructive way, it's important to look at what is missing and find alternative, healthy, positive ways to meet that need.

The Need for Growth

Once the first four fundamental needs are met, we want to have continuous growth. We must constantly grow, evolve, and expand in a multitude of directions, including physically, intellectually, socially, spiritually, and emotionally. As Tony Robbins said, "If a tree is not growing, it's dying." That applies to everything and everyone. If your relationship is not growing, it's dying. If your career is not growing, it's dying.

It's important that we constantly develop and grow in some way. In fact, that is exactly what you're doing right now. By reading this book, you are growing by learning. And we can keep growing by reading, watching educational videos, taking classes, learning new languages, learning about new cultures, and traveling. Traveling is actually the best way to learn and grow.

The Need for Contribution

The sixth and final need is the need for contribution. As we grow and expand, we have the need to contribute to this world. Even if you have a successful career, even if you're making a lot of money, if you're doing it all just for the money without feeling like you're contributing to the world, you will not feel truly fulfilled.

For example, I am meeting my need for contribution right now as a teacher, as a coach, and as a health-care professional. I am sharing my knowledge with you, and I feel that I am contributing to this world. You are meeting this need by being a great parent to your children. Your contribution to this world might be to lead by example.

COACHING TIP

Since we are talking about the six human needs, take a few moments for yourself and complete this quick exercise. For each of the six needs below, make a list of what you do every day, every week, every month, and/or every year to meet this need for yourself. Once you have identified how *you* meet this need for *you*, only then you can figure out how to help your child meet each of these needs. Grab a pencil and complete each of these statements:

1. To meet my need for certainty, I do this every day/week/month/year:
2. To meet my need for variety, I do this every day/week/month/year:
3. To meet my need for love and connection, I do this every day/week/month/year:
4. To meet my need for significance, I do this every day/week/month/year:
5. To meet my need for growth, I do this every day/week/month/year:
6. To meet my need for contribution, I do this every day/week/month/year:

Now look at your answers. Have you left any blanks? If so, those needs are not getting met for you. Think of two or three alternative ways to meet the need that's not fulfilled. What actions can you take today to get that need met? Pick one action and do it by the end of this week. You'll be glad you did.

When Needs Go Unmet

Now let's talk about what happens when the six human needs are not met. When our needs are not met, our expectations are not met, and when our expectations are not met, we feel a sense of loss. This sense of loss leads to pain, which leads to anger or sadness. This all ties back to not being fully and truly aligned with our inner being.

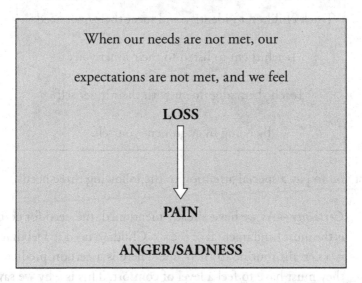

When our needs are not met, our

expectations are not met, and we feel

LOSS

PAIN

ANGER/SADNESS

We discussed in the previous chapter the importance of alignment with our Inner Being, the truest part of who we really are, the extension of source energy. We talked about the idea that we are spiritual beings having a physical (or human) experience. As such, each of us is an extension of source energy trying to create our own reality. Each of us, including our children, wants to create reality that meets all our needs and expectations.

What You Can Do Today

Now that you know what the six human needs are, you can teach your children how to meet their needs and find alignment for themselves. And you can do that by the example of your own alignment. But what does it mean, and how do you do that?

What you can do today is teach your children to be able to identity their needs and then how to meet their needs on their own. Yes, you can be there for them while they're little, but as they grow, they need to learn to identify and meet their own needs.

You must educate them. Teach them to listen to their inner voice. Teach them alignment with their Inner Being, with their inner self, by being aligned yourself. This is the best and the truest way to actually teach someone alignment.

> Teach children to identify and meet their own needs.
>
> Teach them to listen to their inner voice.
>
> Teach them alignment with their inner self
>
> by being in alignment yourself.

I want you to pay a special attention to the following three needs:

- *Certainty*—As we have already mentioned, the need for certainty is the most fundamental of the six. Children need to feel that there is a certain routine to their life. There is a certain predictability they must have to feel a level of comfort. This is why we say that children thrive on routine. Certainty is very important to our kids (as it is to all of us).
- *Love and connection*—Being accepted by their peers, friends, and classmates plays a huge role in our kids' lives. I'm going to give you some pointers, tips, and tricks on what you can do today to help your kids feel connected.
- *Significance*—Kids want to feel special, noticed, and even admired by their peers. They try to fit in, but at the same time, they want to stand out.

These three needs are really big in today's world for our kids, especially for teens and preteens. Helping them meet their needs starts by listening. Someone wise once said, "This is why you have one mouth and two ears." I suppose this explains why we are supposed listen twice as much as we speak.

We need to really listen to understand what our children's needs are, and we must remember those three needs: *Certainty, Connection,* and *Significance.*

To meet the need for certainty, you want to start to educate your child about this need and have an open, honest conversation about how it is met or not met. If you really listen and let children speak without interrupting (no, seriously, shut up and let them talk), they will tell you. You just have to be there. If your relationship is not in a place where your child will easily open up to you, do not push and do not preach. Just be there, patient and open, ready to listen when your child is ready to talk.

Kids these days will use social media to meet their needs for connection and significance, and they will sometimes become obsessed with the number of likes and follows that they have on Snapchat and Instagram and/or other platforms. This has almost become their main source of interaction and connection with others. This is the digital generation, and this is how they operate; don't try to change that. If you do, you'll only disappoint yourself and them.

If you want to keep an eye on them Snapchat-ing or Instagram-ing, you can do that, but don't try to understand or invade—you will only alienate them. You only need to accept it. (Visit the bonus chapter "Your Child and Electronics" in the appendix for more discussion on this topic.) I don't fully understand my kids' worlds, but I can accept that, and I can tell by their behavior if that world is being constructive or destructive to them.

Keep in mind that early sexual activity is directly related to the need for love and connection not being met at home. Children who are not receiving enough hugs, kisses, and words of affirmation at home will look for that love and connection elsewhere. Statistics show that girls get involved in early sex and unprotected sex if they don't get enough hugs, kisses, and I-love-yous at home. This is especially true for girls with ADHD. The same goes for boys.

So make sure to show your kids plenty of physical expression of your affection and praise. Tell them how loved they are. Otherwise, they will look for this affection elsewhere and may do it in unhealthy ways.

The same goes for the need for significance. The selfie culture comes from wanting to be important, wanting to be noticed. Unfortunately, this is also where the culture of entitlement comes from. So what can you do? You want to make your child feel special. You want to praise and thank your child as much as you can. You cannot overappreciate your child.

Sometimes this question comes up with my coaching clients. They say, "I am afraid that I will overcompliment them or overthank them, and they will just grow too proud or arrogant."

My response to that is: "It's not possible." You can never overcompliment someone. People who come across as arrogant act this way because they are compensating for *not* feeling appreciated or special enough. Bullies are bullies because they do not feel appreciated or important outside of their bully–victim relationship. Snobs are snobs because they are compensating for their unmet need for significance.

Certainty, connection, and significance—these are the three most important human needs that I want you to address with your child, because these three usually require the most attention. From there, you can see that there is enough variety in their lives, while the need for growth, which is met through school and through extracurricular activities, takes care of itself.

However, please note that your kids' needs do not include meeting *your* needs. This is one very important lesson we all need to learn and relearn. Our needs are not as important to others as they are to us. If you have a cat like I do, just look at your cat, because your cat can teach you this over and over again. All its body language says to you is: "You will never be as important to me as I am to me." That's kind of how our kids are. That's how most people operate.

We love our children so much, those selfish little brats! But your kids are pretty much like your cat. They will never care about your needs as much as you care about theirs. They will never care about your needs as much as *you* must care about *your* own needs. Therefore, it's your responsibility to meet your needs.

It's not your child's responsibility to make you feel happy and aligned with yourself. It's up to you to do that and find your own alignment with your Inner Being. And that's exactly what we will talk about in the upcoming chapter.

In the meantime, I want to share with you a special strategy I have developed that can help your relationship right away. You can implement it starting today and see the results almost immediately.

Special Bonus Strategy: STARS

I absolutely love this strategy, and I teach it in my relationship coaching practice. I call this my STARS strategy, for its acronym: S, T, A, R, and S.

This strategy is composed of five basic elements—five things you can do on a daily basis to have a beautiful relationship with your child. However, you can also apply this strategy to your relationship with practically anyone, including your spouse, friend, boss, sibling, parent, or anyone you want to improve your relationship with, even yourself.

These are the five things you want to remember to do every single day. You might want to print this out or write it down and put it on your mirror, your fridge, or wherever you can see it regularly. I promise you that if you do these five things every day, your relationship will rise to the next level of wonderful.

So what are the five components of the STARS strategy?

STARS:

- S – Smile
- T – Thank
- A – Align
- R – Respect
- S – Show

S Is for Smile

Smile when you see your kids or greet them for the first time after not seeing them for some time. Be fully present and in the moment as you smile genuinely. This cannot be a fake smile; it must be heartfelt.

This is very important and is often overlooked. When you see your kids for the first time after not seeing them for a while (for example, when you pick them up from school, when they come home, or when you see them first thing in the morning), that greeting, that moment actually, believe it or not, sets the tone for the rest of your time together. How often do we take that for granted and just ignore that moment? Sometimes we don't even look at each other.

I want you to change that. I want you to pay full attention, be fully present, smile, and give all your attention. However, I want to caution you—do not try to smother them with questions the moment you see them. You want to show them that you're sincerely happy to see them and fully present.

Whatever it is you are going through, whatever it is they are going through, I want you to show how genuinely glad you are to see them and just be there, present in that moment for one full minute. Just one full minute. That's all I'm asking. Sixty seconds. Just be there. Be present and attentive.

T Is for Thanks

Thank and compliment your child every day. Thank-yous and compliments (appreciating someone) are completely underrated in our society, and yet they are so important for establishing trust. They fill up your child's emotional bank account and build self-esteem while making your child feel appreciated.

Do this several times a day. If you tend to forget, set a reminder in your phone or get yourself an alarm or some other prompt that reminds you it's time to pay a compliment or say thanks. It could be first thing in the morning when you see your child, or it could be the last thing at bedtime. Either way, you want to compliment and thank your child as much as possible.

When you do that—when you thank or compliment someone sincerely—you release a charge of positive energy and put yourself in the vibration of appreciation and gratitude. Being in this state attracts into your existence more things and events for you to appreciate and be grateful for. It works like magic. So start saying thanks every chance you get.

Find even the smallest things to thank others for or to compliment them on. It can even be physical attributes. For example, "Oh, I like your hair today. It looks nice." Or, "Great outfit—I like that." You can compliment anything positive that you can think of. Remember, compliments show appreciation and benefit both the giver and the receiver.

Find anything positive and say it!

Catch your children in the act of doing something good and praise them for it. If they help you with a household chore or do something nice, say, "Well, thank you so much. It really means a lot to me when you are helping out." You must sound sincere, though. The compliment becomes worthless if it sounds like sarcasm. In fact, it will have the opposite effect. So beware.

Find things your child is good at and say it out loud. It's essentially important. Remember, you cannot overcompliment or overthank somebody. This is the foundation of a beautiful relationship you can have with your kid, especially an ADHD kid whose self-confidence is low. Help to boost that self-esteem with plenty of thanks and compliments.

A Is for Alignment

Focus on being authentically aligned with yourself. Listen to your emotions and use them not to react but as an indicator of your alignment with yourself. When you are experiencing negative emotions, it simply means that you are out of alignment and need to shift your focus to better feelings and thoughts to become more aligned.

This also means letting go. Let go of old expectations and frameworks that no longer serve you and stop complaining. Stop focusing on what you don't want or don't like. Yes, it's important to identify what you don't want or like in order to identify what you *do* want, but it does not serve you to dwell on it.

Stop complaining in general, and stop complaining about your child or your relationship with your child in particular. You see, when you are complaining, you are putting yourself deliberately out of alignment and into the vibrational state of what you do not want.

Instead, focus on the good and what is working (see "T for Thanks"). Think of the moments when you felt good and really concentrate on the feelings those thoughts evoke in you. Let go of things you cannot control and focus on the one thing you can control: your own alignment with yourself.

> ## A Quick Note from Experience: Complaining About Complaining Is Still Complaining
>
> I have a friend who used to call me only to complain about things in his life and work. Whenever I would see his caller ID on my phone, I felt reluctant to pick up, because I knew I would hear some complaining. However, I caught myself and realized that I was complaining about his complaining. As soon as I stopped doing that, he stopped calling me with complaints. Isn't it interesting how that works?

R Is for Respect

Yes, these are kids, but we want to be polite with them too, because that shows respect and kindness. You never want to take anything for granted, so you want to always say please and thank you, hello and goodbye. Always.

This also means stop arguing. We will talk more about this in upcoming chapters—specifically, when we get to the topic of responding versus reacting. For now, just try to catch yourself in the act of arguing and make yourself stop. Take a pause and ask yourself: *Is what I am about to say necessary? Is it kind? Is it polite?*

When in doubt, ask yourself: *Could I say this in the same manner to my boss?* If not, then don't do it to your child or your loved one.

Always be polite and respectful with your child. Remember, you are leading by example. You're teaching kids the way you want them to be in the future with you and their loved ones. So always be polite with them.

Choose the words you use to communicate with your child (and even with yourself) wisely. Remember, your words can change the way you see your world, and the way you see your world becomes your world.

S Is for Show

Show and express the physical affirmation of your affection and respect. Some kids are good with hugs and kisses; others not so much, especially teenagers, as they sometimes distance themselves from their parents. So politely and respectfully (R for Respect) ask, "How may I show my affection with you?" If your child is not comfortable with hugs and kisses, find out what would be comfortable—maybe a pat on the back or a stroke of a shoulder or a squeeze of a hand. It could be just a slight gesture or small touch that shows a physical affirmation of your affection.

My teenage son sometimes does not want me to express affection. When I really want to hug him, I simply open my arms and stand there, waiting for him to come to me with an embrace. And he does practically every time. As your relationship grows and improves, you will see that even teenagers will allow you to hug them more and show more affection.

Special Note

Some children and teens have touch hypersensitivity when it comes to certain textures of various clothing fabrics, which might make hugging uncomfortable. In that case, you may open your arms for a hug (or use other body language) and let them come to you for a hug or other gesture of affection.

For Extra Credit

If you want to go that extra mile, create a mission statement. The mission is you being the best parent you can be. Write it down and then commit to it.

Make it a simple statement. It doesn't have to be long; it can be just a few words as long as it is truthful and feels good. For example, "I want to be the best mom that I can be to my son." That's it. Simple and to the point. Or you could make it, "I am lucky that you are my kid, and I will do anything I can to support you in every way." That's all.

It doesn't have to be long, but come up with a phrase that you can tell your child regularly. This becomes a huge deposit into your child's emotional bank account, and it sets the tone for your entire relationship.

If you are having a hard time saying it out loud, just write your mission statement somewhere on a piece of paper and post it where both of you can see it. You are going to see a positive change, I promise you.

To wrap up this chapter, I want to share with you this quote from K. Heath: "Kids are like a mirror, what they see and hear, they do. Be a good reflection for them."

Key Points

- We all have these six human needs, but our children especially need help in meeting their needs for certainty; love and connection; and significance.
- Make sure to give lots of love to your kids at home.
- Practicing the STARS strategy is an excellent way to help kids meet their needs for certainty; love and connection; and significance.

Step 3
Meet Your Needs

Your kids don't want a perfect mom. They just want a happy one.
—Author Unknown

53

In the last chapter, when we discussed your child's needs, we also mentioned that your child's needs do not include meeting your needs. That's your responsibility. This is what we will focus on here in this chapter.

It is not uncommon for parents to struggle in shifting to meet their own needs, so I hear you. I want you to understand that there is nothing wrong with meeting your own needs. Yes, we often feel guilty about it, and that's very common—especially for moms—but I want you to know that you are not alone.

In this chapter, you will learn how to thrive as a parent, what "to thrive" really means, and the ways you can achieve it.

Here is a quick snapshot of what we're going to cover:

- **First**, we'll talk about your needs and the seven dimensions of wellness.
- **Next**, I'll discuss the neuropsychology of happiness; what it means to survive versus thrive; and how we can shift from a surviving mode into a thriving mode of being.
- **Finally**, I will teach you a special strategy to establish new positive brain patterns and train your brain into a thriving mode, because your brain, just like your muscles, can be trained.

Identifying Your Needs

I want to start this chapter with a quote I found the other day. It just rubbed me the wrong way when I saw it, but I know, unfortunately, that too many people believe it: "Sacrificing your happiness for the happiness of the other person or the one you love, is, by far, the truest type of love."

This could not be further from the truth, and I want to start by explaining to you how wrong this statement is. You see, one can never—and should never—sacrifice one's own happiness and self-alignment for another to feel better. One should never expect this from another person either. We have discussed this before: each person's inner alignment is each person's own responsibility and choice.

I'm going to say that again: happiness is a choice. You cannot make this choice for another person, and others cannot make this choice for you, not even your child.

"Your kids don't want a perfect mom. They just want a happy one." That's the opening quote for this chapter. It means that you need to be happy for your kids' sake, and it's up to you to make the conscious choice to be happy.

Let's begin by addressing your needs—because, as we covered in the previous chapter, when your needs are met, you are happy and satisfied. Yours are the same six human needs that we discussed before. And guess what? When your needs are not met, you feel upset, frustrated, stressed, unhappy, angry, or sad. Again, it's your responsibility, not your child's, to make you happy and meet your needs. Remember, we talked about healthy and unhealthy ways to meet those needs, so choose wisely how you meet your needs.

Your Needs are Important!

The six human needs:

1. Certainty
2. Variety
3. Love and connection
4. Significance
5. Growth
6. Contribution

Now take a moment and honestly answer this question for yourself: Are your needs being met?

Are *all* your needs being met? You may recall a quick exercise in the "Coaching Tip" box in Step 2 chapter. Use it to answer this for yourself.

As we discussed before, when our needs and expectations are not met, we feel pain of loss, which puts us out of alignment with our inner being. Being out of alignment feels like anger, frustration, or sadness. Listen to your emotions. Your emotions are the indicator of your alignment, and your alignment tells you whether your needs are being met.

The Seven Dimensions of Well-Being

I want to take this a step further and talk about the seven dimensions of well-being. I call this the *wheel of wellness*.

These are the seven dimensions of your wellbeing: Physical, Intellectual, Emotional, Spiritual, Social, Financial, and Environmental. Let's expand on each dimension.

1. **Physical**—The physical dimension is obviously your physical well-being—your body, your diet, your exercise routine, and how you take care of your body. These are all part of your physical health.

2. **Intellectual**—The intellectual dimension is all about information processing, critical thinking, memory, decision-making, and the ability to retain information, solve problems, and respond logically.

3. **Emotional**—The emotional dimension includes your emotions and feelings and how you express them. It's your emotional health and your ability to express your feelings in a healthy, mature way.

4. **Social**—The social dimension is all about the relationships in your life and your ability to build good, strong, healthy relationships that are free of condescension or abuse (physical or emotional).

5. **Spiritual**—The spiritual dimension is about your connection to the universe and your alignment with your Inner Being. When we talk about inner alignment, we're talking about your connection with yourself and your connection with nature, a higher being (if you are religious, that would be God), and yourself.

6. **Financial**—The financial dimension is about feeling comfortable financially. It's about being secure and financially stable.

7. **Environmental**—The environmental dimension is about your environment—where you live and work or spend most of your time. Is your home and workplace conducive to your well-being? This dimension involves keeping your place organized, clean, neat, and free of clutter. Some people even apply feng shui principles to their home and/or their place of work because the environmental health dimension is so important.

All seven dimensions are tightly interconnected. When one of the dimensions becomes compromised, the others usually follow. It's important to understand this. For example, when you're not feeling well physically, you are probably not going to feel very well emotionally. When you're not feeling well emotionally, you're probably not going to be able to make clear decisions, and your memory might be affected when you're emotionally down or depressed.

If you are not doing well financially, you're probably going to be affected intellectually, emotionally, and spiritually. When we are not feeling well in any dimension, our ability to socialize and form connections with others may be impacted.

If you have seen the film *P.S. I Love You*, you might recall how the heroine of the story is completely devastated by the death of her husband. In fact, she gets so depressed (emotional dimension) that she becomes physically incapacitated and cannot even get out of her bed (physical dimension). She isolates herself from friends and family in her grief (social dimension). When others come to visit her, they find her apartment a complete mess (environmental dimension).

This shows how all the dimensions of wellness are tightly intertwined. When one is greatly affected, the others follow. Grasping this concept is a necessary step to understanding how to bring all our health dimensions into harmony so we can thrive.

The Tree of Livelihood and Positive Psychology

I want to tell you a story of a man and his Tree of Livelihood. This was a special tree, because it had the magic power to make its caretaker happy. The story goes like this:

> Once upon a time, there was a man, and right outside his house, he had this magic Tree of Livelihood growing. This tree was the reflection of his life and joy, and as long as the tree was growing and green, the man felt happy.
>
> Every morning, this man would come outside and tend to this tree. He would climb up on this tree to

examine every branch and every leaf to make sure that they all looked healthy and green. If any leaves were dehydrated, this man would take a wet sponge and wipe them and moisturize them. He would spend all day just tending to every branch and every leaf. By the end of each day, the man was exhausted, because it took him all day to take care of every leaf. But each morning, he would get up on the tree and start over again, tending to every branch and every leaf.

Looking at this situation from the outside, you would think, "How crazy is that? Why not just water the roots?" However, isn't this what many of us do? We tend to the leaves instead of the roots of the problems in our lives. Each of us has a tree like that, and the roots of that tree are our happiness and fulfillment—the balance and alignment with our Inner Being. By first tending to those roots, we can take care of our entire Tree of Livelihood.

This means that by first working on achieving the alignment with Inner Being, which is the root of our livelihood, we can create a happy and fulfilling life. First, you must feel happy. Then, what you want will come to you. That's what we mean by "tending to the roots." Your alignment is the root of the tree of *your* livelihood.

This is why better results do not lead to more happiness. It's the other way around. Happiness leads to better results.

> ## Tending to the Roots: Positive Psychology
>
> Better results do not lead to happiness.
>
> Happiness leads to better results.

This brings us to the concept of positive psychology, which we will address here briefly. If you look it up, you will find that this field of science, founded by Martin Seligman, studies the strengths that enable us to thrive. Positive psychology is based on the belief that each of us wants to live a meaningful and fulfilling life and to continuously expand and enhance our experience of happiness, love, joy, and fulfillment.

I will make this super simple for the purposes of this book. The whole idea of positive psychology operates on three levels:

1. **Subjective**—our positive experiences, such as love, happiness, optimism, inspiration, and joy
2. **Individual**—where our positive experiences from the subjective level influence our individual human experiences (our material, tangible results)
3. **Community**—where the first two levels allow us to build thriving relationships with others.

The latter two levels are nothing more than manifestations of the expression of the first level.

It's all about understanding what must come first: your priorities. And what must come first is your need to get happy before you can see desired results in life, as results are nothing more than manifestations of joy and fulfillment.

This means that first, you must feel love, joy, and inspiration, and then they will manifest themselves in the material world.

Most people have it backward. How many times have you heard, "When this or that happens, then I'll be happy" from others, or even from yourself? For example:

- "When I get my promotion, then I will be happy."
- "When I lose twenty pounds, then I'll be happy."
- "When my child graduates high school, then I'll be happy."

This does not work, because this is conditional living.

Let's say you received a promotion you have been waiting for, and you feel happy for a few hours or days or even weeks. If your happiness is conditional, you will eventually go back to where you started—your baseline level of life satisfaction.

I was giving a health talk for a group of seniors some time ago. The topic was joint health and arthritis. At the end of my lecture, an elderly lady in the audience raised her hand and said, "I went to my doctor complaining of pain in my knees from arthritis. My doctor said that I should just go and get happy. That's exactly what I did, and the pain is now gone!" This is a perfect example of positive psychology in action.

However, you might say, "But how can I get happy if I have all these problems right now?" This is why we must also understand *cognitive psychology.* Cognitive psychology focuses on the mental process that is essential to the subjective level of positive psychology, which has to do with our positive emotions, such as love, joy, inspiration, and fulfillment.

Here is a quick lesson on cognitive psychology. We're now talking about the intellectual dimension on the wheel of wellness.

Dysfunctional thought processes lead to a dysfunctional life. It's as simple as that. If you want your wheel of wellness to reflect a happy and fulfilling life, you need to start with the intellectual health dimension on that wheel, because you have the ability to choose your own thoughts. Specific thoughts lead to specific emotions, which lead to specific manifestations in the rest of the health dimensions on the wheel of wellness.

Quick Lesson on Cognitive Psychology

Focus on the intellectual health dimension on your wheel of wellness—your thoughts. Remember, dysfunctional thought processes lead to a dysfunctional life.

Since most of us have a constant conversation with ourselves in our heads, we can and must choose the words we use for self-talk. (We will discuss more of this later in the chapter, where I will give you a very specific strategy that you can apply to see positive results right away.) Once we learn to control and choose our own thoughts, our life starts changing for the better. That's what we mean by "tending to the roots" of our Tree of Livelihood.

Surviving versus Thriving

The surviving mode is where we are stressed, angry, frustrated, or sad. In other words, we are misaligned with ourselves as opposed to being in a thriving mode where we are aligned with our inner being. Remember: our emotions are the indicator of our inner alignment.

When we are in this surviving mode, we tend to have tunnel vision, meaning we cannot think outside the box or think creatively to come up with alternative solutions to a given problem. We get stuck in a dark place, and all we can see and all we can think of is the problem that's in front of us. That's all that's in our focus at the time.

Picture a racehorse with blinders on: it can only see what's immediately in front of it. Just like that horse, when we are in surviving mode, we have blinders on. All we can see is the problem in front of us.

I want you to get out of that survival mode.

I want you to take the blinders off so you can start seeing more—start noticing opportunities and solutions you cannot see from survival mode. I want you to get out of tunnel vision so you can go into thriving mode and look at everything differently. When you are in thriving mode, you can approach any situation more creatively. You can think outside the box and see the situation from a different angle, a different perspective, than before.

How do you take the blinders off and get out of tunnel vision? The answer is simple and complex at the same time: find your alignment within. I want you to think of the importance of finding that alignment so you can really start thriving. This would be truly tending to the roots of your Tree of Livelihood.

COACHING TIP

I want you to do this quick exercise called "Top Ten Things I Love to Do."

Take a pencil and fill in the ten blanks below. Come up with ten different activities that make you happy when you are doing them. For example, you could come up with something like this:

- When I read a romance novel, I feel happy.
- When I hug my son, I feel happy.
- When I sing, I feel happy.
- When I bake cookies, I feel happy.

Here is a worksheet you can use, or write these out on a separate sheet:

1. When I (insert a verb) _____, I feel happy.
2. When I (insert a verb) _____, I feel happy.
3. When I (insert a verb) _____, I feel happy.
4. When I (insert a verb) _____, I feel happy.
5. When I (insert a verb) _____, I feel happy.
6. When I (insert a verb) _____, I feel happy.
7. When I (insert a verb) _____, I feel happy.
8. When I (insert a verb) _____, I feel happy.
9. When I (insert a verb) _____, I feel happy.
10. When I (insert a verb) _____, I feel happy.

> Once you have all ten statements completed truthfully, mark the ones you have done over the past week. If you have marked eight out of ten or more things over the past week you love to do, you are generally a happy person. Congratulations! Keep it up! ☺
>
> If you marked seven or less, that means you need more "me" time to tend to your needs. Make an effort to get more than seven of the top ten things you love to do every week and watch the change in how you feel emotionally.

I want you to shift your mode from surviving to thriving. To do that, you need to establish new patterns in your thought process.

Again, water the roots: reframe your perspective and find your alignment. Shift your focus from tending to the leaves to tending to the roots. The leaves will become healthier on their own as the result of this new approach.

What You Can Do Today

Here is what we're going to do starting today. From this point forward, we will begin to rewire your brain. What does that mean?

Our brains have some established neuronal connections—set pathways—which means this: we tend to think in certain patterns, using certain words for self-talk. Certain thoughts evoke certain emotions, which lead to certain manifestations. Today, we're going to change that. Starting now, we will begin to rewire your brain to reprogram your mind with new patterns, new words for self-talk, and new thinking processes. Gradually, you will see that you'll get new results.

Establish New Patterns in Your Thought Process

When we say "rewire your brain," we mean reprogram your mind to think in new ways and directions. A brain, just like muscles, can be trained. You will retrain your brain to build new neuronal connections and pathways (new connections between the nerve cells) so that you can achieve a higher level of wellness in all areas of your life and reach fulfillment. You can become not only happier but also a more effective parent to your child.

If you change your focus, you will change your world. Your focus determines your reality. Are you ready? I'm going to teach you this special brain rewire strategy right now.

Brain Rewire Strategy

This simple strategy starts with becoming mindful of your thought patterns. Start paying attention to the thoughts you are thinking. Start observing and noticing how your thoughts influence your emotional state. What words are you using in your mind? Pay attention to your thought patterns and become more mindful of your own self-talk.

Start observing and noticing your thoughs. Are they focused in the future? Are they taking you back to the past? Once you become more aware of your own thought patterns, you will notice that the majority of your anxiety-driving thoughts come from the unknown future, and most of your angry or sad thoughts come from the past.

Switch from Negative to Neutral

When you notice a negative thought, switch to a neutral thought and get into the present moment. What does that mean?

It's almost impossible to immediately switch from a negative thought to a positive one. It's like trying to make a U-turn while going eighty miles an hour. There is too much momentum going in the opposite direction of where you want to go—too much momentum in the negative thought and emotion. Instead of doing a full U-turn, what you want to do is slow down, switch to neutral, and then start turning things around.

When I say *neutral*, I mean a neutral feeling thought—anything that is off the topic. A great way to get off the negative topic and switch to neutral is to return to the present moment. Be right here, right now.

As we mentioned earlier, most of our negative thoughts come from either the past or the future. Most of our disappointments, anger, or sadness come from the past. Most of our anxieties come from the uncertain future. What we want to do is get out of the past and out of the future and into the present moment.

The easiest way to get back into the present moment is to take a deep breath and observe yourself for a few seconds: observe your body, your face, how you are sitting or standing. Pretend that you're looking at yourself from a different corner of the room from where you are and just watch yourself be.

Try that right now. Take a deep breath and spend the next few seconds pretending that you are looking at yourself from a different vantage point. This grounds you immediately and puts you in the present moment. To also help put yourself into the present, you can look around at your surroundings and notice the sounds around you.

If you are indoors, notice sounds outside. Notice the temperature of the room, the sensations in your body, in your face, in your toes and fingertips. What are you hearing, seeing, smelling? Are you cold or warm? What is your facial expression right now? What is your body's physical position?

Shift Your Physical State

Science shows that when you do a quick cat stretch, your brain releases endorphins, which make you feel good. Endorphins also lower our perception of pain and make us feel happier. Stretch to shift your body's physical position, and that will help shift your physical state, which can lead to a shift in your emotional state as well.

Tony Robbins, a life coach I greatly admire, said that if you want to change your emotional state, you must first notice it and make a conscious choice to change it. Then, to change your emotional state, you must change your physical state. The fastest way to do that is to change your posture.

As soon as you notice a negative thought, bring yourself into the present moment by taking a few seconds to observe yourself, and then change your position: sit up straight, stand, take a deep breath and stretch, or get into a Superman pose—whatever works for you, but change that posture. Change that body position.

Try this right now: stand or sit up straight, take a deep breath, and do a quick stretch while pretending that you are looking at yourself from another corner of your space. You are now in the neutral zone of your thoughts and emotions, and you are ready to move into a better-feeling thought.

Say your Self-Affirmation Statement

Once you are neutral and in the present, use a self-affirmation statement to move to a better-feeling thought. Right now, let's come up with a simple statement you can tell yourself. This will be your self-affirmation statement or power statement. It is a statement that reminds you that everything is good and working out the best possible way for you.

The following are some examples of self-affirmation statements:

- "Everything is working out the best possible way for me right now and always."
- "I am feeling better and better every day."
- "Things I want are coming to me at the right time through the right channels."
- If you're religious, you could use, "God and my guardian angels love and support me now and forever."
- If you are spiritual but not religious, you could use, "I am in harmony with myself and my universe. My universe supports me and takes care of me."

Take a few minutes to brainstorm and figure out your self-affirmation statement—a simple short phrase that works for you to remind you of the deeper, greater purpose behind what you really want (inner alignment and peace).

When I struggle with my kids, I use the self-affirmation statement, "I am being the best mom that I can be, and all I have to do is keep loving them. I am doing well and getting better and better every day."

Your self-affirmation statement must have two important attributes: first, whatever phrase you come up with for yourself must feel true to you, and second, it must feel good to you. Feel true and feel good—those are the two requirements you'll want from your self-affirmation statement.

So put this book aside for a few minutes, do some brainstorming, and come up with a perfect phrase or statement that you can use for this step. This is your self-reassurance statement, something that reminds you that you are okay and everything's going to be okay. Maybe that could be your phrase. You could say, "Everything is okay. Everything is working out for me the way it should."

Practice Your Statement Every Day

Whatever power phrase you want to use, write it down on a piece of paper, memorize it, and practice saying it to yourself every day, several times a day. At first, I want you to practice this on purpose. This means that every day, at least twice daily, you're going to purposefully go through the actions above. The stretch you do will help you anchor the feeling of power and self-reassurance from your self-affirmation statement. So, in the future, every time you take a stretch and say to yourself that statement, you will anchor the new feeling deeper and deeper into your subconscious until it becomes automatic.

As you train your brain to do this on purpose, you will notice that, gradually, your thought patterns will start changing toward more positive pathways. Then later, even in negative situations, you will find yourself more balanced and emotionally in control and start responding more positively.

Note: some people may have to do more work, or even work with a therapist, to break the cycle of negative thinking and being triggered, especially if there has been a history of abuse or trauma. In this case, hypnotherapy, coaching, or other sources of healing or training may be useful. Some people find the emotional freedom technique (a.k.a. tapping), which can be done without a therapist, beneficial in breaking the trigger cycle of a negative thinking process.

My brain-rewire strategy will allow you to reclaim your power over your thoughts, your emotions, and your feelings, which will in turn shape your reality. You are the BOSS of your own life, and this is the BOSS strategy.

> ## Brain-Rewire Strategy:
>
> # BOSS
>
> **B**—Breathe
>
> **O**—Observe
>
> **S**—Stretch
>
> **S**—Self-Affirmation

In the BOSS strategy for brain rewiring, the *B* stands for *breathe*; you are reminded to take a deep breath and get yourself into the present moment, which is immediately followed by the *O* for *observe*. This means stop and observe yourself and your surroundings. Try to really notice the details and use all your senses. This puts you further into the present moment.

Next is taking a quick *stretch*, which is the first *S* in BOSS. This makes your body release endorphins, the happy brain chemicals, and puts you even further into the present, taking you out of the past or the future. Stretch as you repeat your *self-affirmation* statement in your mind, which is the last *S* in the acronym. As you say it and take your stretch at the same time, you are anchoring (connecting the positive emotion to the stretch) these actions together.

Memorize that self-affirmation statement. Repeat it every time you practice the BOSS tool or whenever you feel a negative thought or emotion. Keep doing this every day. Keep practicing the BOSS strategy until you feel that you have become the boss of your own feelings and thoughts, and then keep doing it for the rest of your life. Set reminders for yourself or link the practice to routines you already do every day. For example, you can link it to when you brush your teeth in the morning and in the evening. Go through the BOSS sequence at those times.

Keep repeating this and keep practicing it. Think of it as training for your brain, like an exercise you do regularly. After some time, your brain will get rewired to follow the newly established pattern. As you keep practicing, you will get better and better at mastering your emotional state. It's going to get easier and easier. And you will be able to switch off the negative thoughts before they gain momentum, I promise.

By the way, I can't wait to hear what self-affirmation statement you come up with. Please write to me at coachgelena.com. I really want to see and hear what your self-affirmation statement is. Just remember, "If you change your thoughts, you will change your world."

When we change our thoughts, it means we're choosing different words for how we talk to ourselves. The words we choose create how we see our world. And how we *see* our world *becomes* our world.

That's what I want for you: I want you to create your own world, your own reality, from the place of your alignment. I want you to make this choice today, I want you to make this decision right now. Promise to yourself that you're going to be happy no matter what, because happiness is a choice. Choose wisely.

BE HAPPY!

(no matter what)

To wrap up this lesson, I want to quote Andy Smithson: "The sign of great parenting is not the child's behavior. The sign of truly great parenting is the parent's behavior." So be happy, and everything else will come.

Key Points

- You are the only person responsible for meeting your needs. Nobody else can do it for you, and meeting your needs starts with your mind-set. Your mind-set is the root of your livelihood.
- There are seven dimensions of wellness that are tightly interconnected: physical, intellectual, emotional, social, spiritual, environmental, and financial. When one suffers, the rest follow.
- To achieve balance, we must start with the intellectual dimension of wellness to rewire the thinking process from a surviving to a thriving mode of being. Then the rest of the dimensions will follow.

- When you focus on your inner alignment, you naturally turn from survival mode to a thriving mode of being.
- Rewire your brain for thriving by choosing thoughts that feel good. Practice the BOSS strategy every day, several times a day, to help rewire your brain for alignment: take a deep *b*reath, *o*bserve yourself and your surroundings, *s*tretch, and say your *s*elf-affirmation statement. It only takes a few seconds and costs nothing, but the results will astonish you in the long run.

Step 4
Learn to Respond, Not React

If children are always performing in order to obtain something—
good grades, or awards, or praise, from teachers or parents—
then they don't get to develop their inner drive.
—Jessica Alexander

You are doing great moving through the chapters. So far, we have completed step 1, reframe the situation; step 2, understand your child's needs; and step 3, meet your needs. In that third step, we shifted your mode of being from surviving to thriving, and we did it by finding your alignment and using the BOSS strategy to rewire your brain. I really hope you have started practicing BOSS by now.

Remember, you can apply that strategy when experiencing any negative triggers and whenever you feel out of alignment. Once you're in thriving mode, you are more likely to make positive responses. Only then are you ready for this chapter. Step 4 involves becoming an effective communicator by responding instead of reacting. Here is a quick snapshot of what we're going to cover:

- **First**, I will define the difference between responding versus reacting.
- **Next**, we will talk about the importance of really listening and responding to kids instead of just talking *at* them. You have probably noticed that many times when you talk to your child, your words are not getting through, as if they are just bouncing back. That's the case when you are talking *at* instead of *to* your child. We are going to talk about how to speak so that your child is receptive to your words.
- **Then**, we will talk about choosing your focus when communicating with your child. It's important to keep the right focus in mind. I will give you real and practical tips you can apply right now and

see results immediately. I will give you specific things to say and do in two common scenarios. I will show you what you need to do when you feel upset, or in other words, when you're out of alignment.

- **Finally**, we'll discuss what to do when your child (or another person) feels upset. Let's face it: this will happen. People get upset every so often. Even the most calm, harmonious, and aligned people in the world, like the Dalai Lama, probably experience such moments every now and then. After a while, you will see that as you keep practicing the strategies I'm teaching you in this book, you will have less and less out-of-alignment moments.

Respond or React?

We discussed before how children enter this world to create their own reality. So we must let them practice creating theirs while we practice creating ours. While we work on creating our own reality and try to control our own circumstances, we may be reacting or responding to the changes in our environment and the very reality we create. But what does that mean? What is the difference between reacting and responding?

Reacting is usually quick and emotional. It can be aggressive or tense without giving much thought to the event or the consequences. It's an emotional knee-jerk reflex to an irritating stimulus. In many cases, reacting provokes reaction in another, which perpetuates emotional discord during a given interaction. Just think of the last time you observed a bickering fight between two young siblings. It's a back-and-forth exchange (usually emotional) that escalates to the point of someone getting hurt.

Responding, on the other hand, is rather calm, logical, thought out, and peaceful. It comes from a place of logic, confidence, and alignment. Here is an old story I want to share with you that perfectly illustrates reacting versus responding:

> An executive of a large company was angry and yelled at one of his directors. The director became upset, went home, and yelled at his wife for overspending. The wife got upset and yelled at the maid for breaking a dish; then

the maid got upset and kicked the dog. The dog ran outside and bit a woman walking by. When this woman went to the clinic, she yelled at the doctor for giving her a painful injection. The doctor went home upset and yelled at his mother. The mother turned around and said, "I am sorry you had a rough day. I know you are tired. Let me run you a bath and make your bed so you can get a good night's rest and feel better in the morning." At this moment, the cycle of anger was broken. It was broken by love, patience, and forgiveness.

With that, let me ask you this question: Do you more frequently react to situations or do you respond to them? If you feel triggered or emotional after certain interactions, which is very typical for most people, that's reacting. However, I want you to know that you are not alone. Every so often we all react emotionally, and it's normal. We're human beings. But remember: our emotions are simply the indicator of our inner alignment. That's all they are. It's important to pay attention to that indicator and use that information to adjust your thoughts and behavior patterns (see Step 3 chapter).

Let's say you're driving your car, and you look down at you dashboard and notice that your gas tank is close to empty. Do you get upset with it? Do you ignore it? Do you cover it with a smiley-face sticker to make it look more attractive? No, of course not! It's just an indicator—a piece of information. And you usually know exactly what to do about it: stop at a gas station and get more gas.

It's the same thing with your emotions. If you find yourself on the negative side of your emotional scale, if you're angry, sad, frustrated, or desperate—in other words, misaligned—you now know that it's just an indicator. You know what you need to do. You can apply strategies and tools from this book (STARS, BOSS, and coaching tips) to do something about it.

I want you to ask yourself this question: What do you prefer from others when they interact with you? Do you want them to react emotionally to you, or do you want them to respond rationally in a calm, reasonable fashion? In most cases, the answer is pretty clear. You probably want people to respond to you instead of reacting. Feeling triggered and reacting emotionally is completely normal, but it's important to understand that it comes from misalignment.

For example, when an interaction with another person elevates you and causes you to feel good about yourself, you are aligned with your Inner Being when interacting with that person. Your Inner Being, remember, wants only harmony and love. It feels good to be aligned with that part of yourself. When you interact with people who allow that alignment to happen, when they elevate you, when they make you feel appreciated, when they make you feel happy, it feels good, right? It's because that puts you more in alignment with yourself.

The opposite happens if an interaction with another person makes you feel emotionally negative or misaligned. For example, if you have an interaction with a person who causes you to feel guilty, angry, sad, ashamed, or inadequate in any way—which makes you feel out of alignment and out of sync with the part of you that wants harmony, love, and good—of course, that feels emotionally uncomfortable.

COACHING TIP

Think of an emotional trigger—a pet peeve, if you will, something that always pushes your buttons or rubs you the wrong way. Think of the last time you encountered it and answer the following questions:

- This trigger caused you to feel a certain emotional pain, which is why you reacted to it. Can you identify the source of that pain?
- Underneath pain there is loss. What is the loss that triggered this reaction? Is it a loss of expectation? A loss of your sense of security? Sense of significance? Sense of connection?
- Underneath pain and loss there is fear. What are you afraid of? Are you afraid of another loss? Is it fear of abandonment? Fear of uncertainty? Fear of death?
- Underneath fear there is usually vulnerability, which comes from your openness, which comes from a place of love. Really focus on that place within yourself; appreciate it and cherish it. Picture it. That's the core of who you are, the most beautiful essence of your humanity. Visualize this essence of you as a beautiful bright light that makes you glow from within. What color is this light? Is it warm? See this light expand and fill up your whole body.
- Next, focus on the sensations in your body. Is that trigger causing any tension in your body? Where is it? If you could visualize it, what shape and color would it be? Focus all your attention on it. Now, visualize that you are using your hands to scoop up that tension from your body and throw it into a bonfire, where it's burned to ashes.

> - Now refocus on the sensations in your body. Is the tension still there? If yes, then repeat the step in the paragraph above. Keep repeating until the tension is completely gone.
>
> Once the tension is gone, go back to visualizing the bright light that makes you glow from within. Watch it grow beyond the contours of your body, expanding out, filling up your room. Hold this image in your mind for a full minute until you feel blissful. You can do this visualization exercise whenever you feel tense or triggered by any event or personal interaction. Have fun with it!

Remember from Step 1 Chapter that misalignment leads to a sense of loss and pain, and that's what we experience. If you think of interactions that caused misalignment with your Inner Being—meaning they made you feel "not enough" in one way or another—all of these interactions have one thing in common: one or both people in this interaction are saying, between the lines, "I want you to change your behavior so that I can feel better, so that I can feel my alignment." Or, alternatively, "You want me to change my behavior so that you can feel better, but I really don't want to do this."

Neither of these work, because if you have to change your behavior so that others feel better, or they have to change their behavior so you can feel better, both cannot achieve inner alignment. Who wins here? Of course, no one.

Remember, it's your responsibility to align with your own Inner Being and your children's responsibility to align with theirs. You can't expect your children to change their behavior so that you can feel more aligned, and vice versa. That's the bottom line. (Read more on that in the bonus chapter entitled "Clean Your Room" in the appendix.)

If you cannot help *your* alignment with *your* Inner Being, you cannot help *their* alignment with *their* Inner Being. Remember, each one of us has to find that alignment for ourselves. So here are the steps I want you to try instead. I want you to make a decision today that you will feel good no matter how your child behaves.

Repeat this phrase: "I will feel good no matter how my child behaves."

First of all, remember, we agreed at the end of the previous chapter—when you made that conscious decision—that you're going to be happy no matter what. Today, I want you to make a conscious decision that you're going to feel good about yourself no matter how your child behaves. Then, once you have made that decision, you are ready to make positive responses, even in situations that may seem negative at first. You can respond in a more creative manner, and your inner calm can set the stage for positive outcomes in your interactions.

A positive response to even negative events can lead to positive outcomes. Once you have made the decision that you will feel good no matter how your child behaves, you can start using positive responses to negative events, and that can lead to positive outcomes. No matter how painful the situation may initially seem, you will always be able to find the silver lining. I'm going to show you exactly how you can do this.

What You Can Do Today

Two Questions

When you find yourself in a situation where you feel upset—in other words, you are misaligned with your Inner Being—I want you to stop and ask yourself these two very important questions.

Question 1: Which of My Six Human Needs Is Not Being Met?

Think about this and ask yourself:

- What is really behind my current hurt?
- What is it that's missing?
- Which need is not being met right now?

- Am I feeling hurt because my need for love and connection is not being met?
- Am I feeling upset because my need for significance is not being met, or is my need for variety not being met?

Let's say your husband promised that you were going to go to the movies, and you were looking forward to that because you hadn't been out of the house for a while. You wanted something different. You wanted to change the scenery. Then he came home late because he was stuck at work, and you ended up not going to the movies after all. You might get upset with your husband because he was not there to go out with you. But what was really behind the pain of unmet expectation was the unmet need for variety. That need was not being met.

Here's another example. Let's say you want your teenager to help you with the dishes, but instead she is sitting and watching YouTube and totally ignoring your request. If it makes you feel uneasy or upset (misaligned), you want to ask yourself: which of my needs is not being met at this time?

Once you have identified what need is not met, then I want you to ask yourself, "How else can I meet this need?" which is the second question you want to ask yourself.

Question 2: What Do I Really Want in This Moment?

Remember, it's your responsibility to meet your needs, no one else's. No one's behavior should affect the way you feel. Remember that. The questions I want you to ask yourself are, "What do I really want right now?" and "How can I get it myself?"

For example, back to the teenager not doing the dishes as she was asked. If your teenager is watching videos instead of helping you with the dishes and you decide that what you *really* want is to feel connection with your child, then leave the dishes for now and sit down with your kid and watch those videos together. Watch YouTube with her for just a little bit. The dishes can wait. No, really, they can wait.

This is what you do when you find yourself out of alignment: figure out what need is not being met and what you really want. Going back to the example of the husband who didn't come home in time to go to the movies, if it was the need for variety that was not being met, you could find other ways to meet that need.

Remember we talked about that in step 2 when we discussed the six human needs and the healthy and unhealthy ways to meet them. You can find an alternative and creative way to meet your need for variety. You can rent a movie, try a different food, prepare a new recipe, or read a new book—anything different that breaks the routine a bit.

If it was your need for love and connection that was not met, then you need to figure out a way to get that love and connection need met for yourself. You can never really rely on another person to do it for you. Yes, you can absolutely make a request. You can ask, but you cannot fully rely and depend on another person to meet your needs for you.

Two Answers

We talked before about teaching kids to find alignment, and we talked about teaching them to identify their needs; that will come with time and practice. It will come as you practice your alignment. Your child will gradually learn by observing you being in alignment yourself. We are going to talk more about this in the next chapter.

For now, let's talk about what you can do when your child is acting up—in other words, when your child is out of alignment. You can apply this very simple strategy to your interactions with anyone when they become emotionally triggered. When people are in a state of anger, frustration, or despair (out of alignment), it is futile to use logic or try to rationalize with them in that moment. They are not receptive to reasoning in that emotional state until they calm down. So here is what you need to do instead. Practice saying these two things.

Answer #1: Okay, I understand

The first is very simple but very important. You must stop yourself from engaging in arguing, no matter how badly you want to offer your opinion or your objection on the subject matter (if they want to know your opinion, they will ask you for it). Bite your tongue and simply say, "Okay, I understand."

That's it. Say it and then shut up and wait to see how they respond. They might be shocked at first by such a response from you, especially if they are used to you arguing back, trying to convince them of something, or replying with buts, ifs, or maybes.

Just a quick note for ladies here. This little phrase, "Okay, I understand," is a fantastic argument stopper, and not only with children. It actually works on anyone, especially men. When they try to say something emotional or argumentative, do not engage. Instead, say, "Okay, I understand."

If arguments are an issue in your household, I promise this will stop them, and that's actually the first thing you need to do. You must stop fighting. These three words stop any argument in its tracks. Try it. It works like magic. And this next thing you will say will make it even better.

Answer #2: What Can I Do to Make You Feel Better?

Your child might not expect this from you. In fact, if such behavior is not typical in your household, your family might be shocked to hear it at first. When you say, "What can I do to make it better?" your child might not have an answer right away and might keep complaining and expressing anger or frustration. All *you* need to do is just keep repeating, "Okay, I understand. What can I do to make it better?"

If your child keeps complaining and keeps venting, you keep repeating, "Okay, I understand. What can I do to make it better?" You will see that your child will start calming down and thinking creatively about, really, what you *can* do to make it better. The first response might be, "Nothing. You can't do anything right now." Then you just reply, "Well, if you can think of something that I can do for you, then I'm here." That's it.

I have a teenage son, and sometimes he would get upset about things (school, tennis, drama at school, his sister, etc.), and then he would vent about his problem in frustration. I would respond, "Okay, I understand. What can I do to make it better?" At first, he wouldn't offer much of a solution, or he would just bark back, "Nothing. You can do nothing."

But I noticed that after a while, if I gave him a few minutes to calm down, he would come up with something that I *could* actually do to make him feel better. It could be something as simple as, "Let's go get Thai food together," or even something silly, but he would start thinking creatively. And his mood shifted as his thought pattern shifted. It works! It's amazing.

If he decides that there is really nothing that I can do for him, then at least he feels that I am on his side and that I genuinely wanted to help him. It is very important for our kids to feel supported by their parents, no matter what. We are there to help meet their need for certainty, significance, and love and connection, remember? We discussed this in Step 2.

If you do these things, you will be practicing your inner alignment as well.

When your focus is in the right place, you are more likely to respond, not react. When others get misaligned, you do not want to join them in *their* misalignment. Instead, you need to focus on your own alignment, which is the right place of focus to begin with. Only then can you properly respond instead of reacting emotionally.

Love and Acceptance

So the takeaway message here, and the key to successful communication, and my message for you in this lesson is this: love and accept yourself just the way you are. Then love and accept your children just the way they are.

I know this is not simple or easy. It takes practice, and it takes rewiring your brain by practicing the new way of thinking every day, which you are now doing as you are using the strategies from this book. As you keep practicing and using these strategies, it will become easier and easier every day, and your relationship with your spirited child will get better and better and better.

Write the following down on a piece of paper:

Let yourself be yourself.

Let them be themselves.

Hang this on your fridge, or on your mirror, or over your desk—wherever you can see it every day so you can remind yourself that it's okay for you to be just the way you are, and it's also okay for them to be just the way they are. Let yourself be yourself, and let them be themselves. That's the key to any successful relationship.

Now, to wrap this up and conclude this chapter, I want to share with you a quote from Kevin Hart: "As your kids grow, they may forget what you said, but won't forget how you made them feel."

Key Points

- We all react emotionally every now and then, but your emotional state is the reflection of your inner alignment or lack thereof. We are more likely to react emotionally when we are out of alignment.
- When you are aligned, you are more balanced, and you are more likely to respond in a kind and loving way, even in a stressful or difficult situation.
- When you feel out of alignment, it's because one or more of your needs is not being met. You need to ask yourself, *Which need is not being met, and how can I meet this need for myself through alternative ways?* Then do that.
- When your child is out of alignment, do not engage at the emotional level. Logical reasoning with upset people does not work either, as they are not receptive in that state. Instead, remember to say, "Okay, I understand. What can I do to make it better?" Keep repeating this until your child calms down.

Step 5

Become a True Leader (Not a Manager)

The challenge of parenting lies in finding the balance between nurturing, protecting, and guiding on one hand, while allowing your child to explore, experiment, and become independent on the other.
—Jane Nelson

I hope you have been applying and practicing the strategies you have been learning in the chapters of this book. By now, you have quite a few tools in your toolbelt. So let's review what we have covered so far in the previous lessons. In step 1, we talked about reframing the situation, specifically reframing ADHD from disorder to neurodiversity. In step 2, we addressed understanding your child's needs and covered the six human needs. In step 3, we discussed meeting your needs, and in step 4, we talked about learning to respond instead of react.

In this chapter, we move on to the fifth and final step: becoming a true leader of your household, your family, and ultimately, your own life. Here we will define what makes a great leader, and why you must become one now. Here is a quick snapshot of what we're going to cover:

- **First**, we will discuss the habits of true leaders.
- **Next**, we will talk about responding to situations and people as a leader (instead of as a manager) to get the results you want. Remember, last time we talked about responding instead of reacting, so here we are taking this to the next level—the level of leading.
- **Then**, I will introduce a special strategy developed by Magali Peysha, CEO and founder of the Center for Strategic Intervention: the four animal prototypes of communication styles everyone can relate to. We will talk about what you can do when you get stuck in one or the other mode of communication, and what you can

do when your child (or another person) communicates in one of those styles.

- **Finally**, we will define the true leader's EEE and how to apply it today.

What Makes a Great Leader?

We talked about this before: children come into this world to create their own reality, and your job as their parent and leader is to nurture them while empowering them to create their own reality. That's what leadership is all about, and that's what we will discuss here.

Let's start with this question: what are the qualities of a great leader? Take a moment and think about this—and while you're thinking, let's ask one of the best and most profound leaders of our times, Nelson Mandela.

True Leaders Really Listen

When Nelson Mandela was interviewed by a reporter, he was asked this very same question: what are the qualities of a great leader? In response, he told a story of his own father, a tribal chief. When the tribe had to get together and make a decision about something important, they would gather in a circle, and each member of the tribe would speak, offer an opinion, propose a solution, or make a comment.

The chief would remain silent until all had spoken. He listened to them all, and only after everyone finished talking did he finally speak his mind. So Mandela said that *listening* is one of the most important skills of a great leader, and we all must learn that skill now. For that, we must stop talking and start listening.

True Leaders Inspire, Not Just Manage

The second important quality of a true leader is to be able to respond in a positive way instead of reacting. And we talked about that in the previous chapter, so by now you should have got that part down pretty well.

You see, we do everything to either avoid pain or get pleasure. These are the two biggest motivators in our lives. For example, you may go to the gym to avoid gaining weight, which would make you feel bad about your self-image (that would be avoiding pain), or you may go to the gym because you love the way you feel after a workout and it makes you feel good about yourself (that would be getting pleasure).

Which of these two options do you think is more effective and attractive? Which would have longer-lasting effects? Before you answer this for yourself, I want to tell you a fable from Aesop called "The Sun and the Wind." The story goes like this:

The Sun and the Wind got into an argument about which one of them was more powerful.

The Wind said: "I am more powerful because I move clouds and cause thunder and lightning. I bring rain and snow, I can even break down trees and houses with hurricanes and tornadoes."

The Sun said: "I am more powerful, because I make everything grow. I make the flowers bloom and the birds sing. Without me, life on earth would be impossible."

It was a lovely autumn afternoon, and this argument went on and on without resolution. Then the Sun and the Wind noticed a lonely traveler walking across the field, and they decided to make a bet: whichever one took the cape off this traveler would be the winner and named the most powerful one.

First, the Wind went to work and started blowing and blowing, trying to tear that cape off the traveler. But the harder the Wind blew, the tighter the traveler would hold on to his cape. Eventually, the Wind gave up.

Then the Sun came out, and the Sun made everything beautiful, warm, and pleasant. The birds started singing, the clouds cleared up, and it became so nice, and so warm, that the traveler took off that cape himself.

Now take a moment and think: which one, the Sun or the Wind, was more effective? Which took more effort and energy? Which do you want to be like? Do you want to be like the Wind, or do you want to be like the Sun?

You see, when we discipline our kids, we usually do it like the Wind or like the Sun. Just think about it. Disciplining like the Wind does not work long-term. It only teaches children to mind you as their manager. And usually, the harder you push, the more your child resists. Eventually, such discipline methods may become too painful, and your child might simply shut down, stop participating in communication, and stop talking to you—or rebel and do something out of spite just to show you that you are not in control. So, with that in mind, make your choice today: do you want to manage like the Wind, or do you want to lead like the Sun? Inspire and support, like the Sun, or push and control, like the Wind?

True Leaders Practice Effective Communication

As the leader of your family, you now realize how important it is to truly listen, to lead from a place of love and kindness, and to inspire others (especially your children) to be the best they can be. However, sometimes you may run into communication roadblocks where you feel unheard, misunderstood, or even ignored. That's where this next section will be useful.

The Four Animal Prototypes

In strategic intervention coaching, we distinguish four animal prototypes of communication styles that I want to share with you here. This strategy was developed by my teacher and the author of *The Strategic Intervention Handbook*, Magali Peysha. I personally find knowing and understanding these four prototypes to be very helpful when communicating with other people.

The four animal prototypes for communication styles are a ram, a grasshopper, a turtle (or snapping turtle), and a dog. It's interesting to notice, though, that we may act as one prototype in one situation or with one person and a different prototype with another.

> ### The Four Main Animal Prototypes of Communication Styles
>
> 1. Ram
> 2. Grasshopper
> 3. Turtle (Snapping Turtle)
> 4. Dog
>
> Try to identify with each. You may be one type in one situation and another in a different situation.)

Again, in different situations, we may communicate like different prototypes. For example, I know I am a dog with my children most of the time, but when I need something done, I turn into a ram, and if I am uncomfortable or upset, I usually become a turtle. Let's take a look at each of these prototypes in detail.

Prototype 1: The Ram

Rams are ...

- ambitious
- creative
- decisive
- successful
- organized
- honest
- overachievers
- not shy
- not afraid to overcommunicate

People who act like rams, for the most part, are ambitious, organized, creative, and honest. You know you are talking to a ram if you notice that this individual is repeating the same things or making the same request or complaint over and over again. This is the ram's signature behavior.

It's rare for kids with ADHD to act like a ram, but they might do that in certain situations, such as when they get hyperfocused on something of special interest. You may notice that you (or someone else in your family or friends) may act like a ram sometimes. Every now and then, I find myself acting like a ram. Sometimes my son Sam can turn into a ram when he gets upset about something.

When Speaking with Rams

- Make sure that they know that you have heard them.
- Repeat what they are saying back to them.
- The reason they keep repeating things again and again is because they think they have not been heard or understood.

You can recognize a ram by repetitive requests or complaints, and you can use this information to your advantage. The reason rams keep repeating things over and over is because they think they have not been heard or their point has not been understood. Make sure that they know you have heard them. Repeat what they are saying back to them. We call this the parrot method—just say back to them what they are telling you.

Take time by responding, "Let me make sure I understand what you are saying …" Take notes so they can see that you are hearing them and taking seriously what they are trying to communicate. Try saying, "Let's write this down and make a plan." Rams react well to organization, planning, and being heard.

If you realize that you are the one acting like a ram, you need to stop and back off. You are probably bulldozing the other person, and most likely, you are doing it because one of your needs is not being met. Recognize which need must be addressed and think of alternative ways to meet this need for yourself. If you really feel that the other person is not hearing you, simply ask them to say back to you what they heard. This can help both you and them to clarify what it is you are trying to communicate.

It is interesting to note that oftentimes in communications between two people, if one person turns into a ram, the other turns into a turtle or a grasshopper.

Prototype 2: The Grasshopper

> ## Grasshoppers ...
>
> - avoid conflict
> - jump away as soon as there is confrontation or an uncomfortable situation
> - can jump away mentally or behaviorally
> - may use distraction or entertainment to soothe themselves
> - take themselves to an easier place that's more fun

Grasshoppers generally have a positive outlook on life situations. They try to avoid conflict by hopping away to something else or escaping the situation physically, mentally, or emotionally. As soon as there is a confrontation, grasshoppers might grab their phone and start checking their messages, visit their social media account, flip on the TV, or start listening to music. Or they might suddenly "remember" that they have something else they need to do urgently and leave.

ADHD kids and adults can turn into grasshoppers when intimidated or pushed. This is their way of escaping difficult situations they do not want to deal with. Of course, this may leave the other person (you, for example) frustrated, especially when tasks, projects, or opportunities get dropped by this escapism behavior of a grasshopper.

> ## When Speaking with Grasshoppers
>
> - Talk in a calm, relaxed setting.
> - Ask to set a time to talk about the topic at hand.
> - Speak in a cheerful way.
> - Keep it light.
> - Give them the confidence and reassurance that you can talk it out without pain or conflict.

If you realize that you are talking to a grasshopper and notice that the individual is looking to escape, know this: grasshoppers need to feel safe and interested in order to stay focused. This may be a challenge when speaking with your ADHD child who prefers grasshopper escapism, but there are certain things you can do.

First, make sure to address your grasshopper in a calm, light, and cheerful manner in a relaxed setting (for example, while watching TV, taking a walk, or playing a game). Make them feel safe by making it known in advance that you can talk it out without conflict or pain. Schedule an appointment with them (ask when would be a good time) to talk about the issue you want to address so your grasshopper can mentally prepare for it.

If you notice yourself being a grasshopper in any given interaction, stop and ask yourself: *What am I really avoiding and why? Is there a pain point I am avoiding? Which one of my needs is not being met?* Ask to reschedule this important conversation to a time when you feel that you and the other person can discuss the issue in a calm and productive manner so you can mentally and emotionally prepare for it.

My daughter Abi can be a grasshopper when it comes to doing homework or some household chores, or anything she does not like to do. However, when things get serious and she feels really intimidated (especially by a ram), she turns into a turtle—and if she is pushed continually, she becomes a snapping turtle. This is actually a very typical scenario: when one person becomes a ram, the other turns into a turtle and simply hides within by shutting down.

Prototype 3: The Turtle (Snapping Turtle)

Turtles ...

- are slow-moving
- are all about protection and feeling safe
- take shelter within
- wait out emotions by going internal
- may feel like shrinking down to wait things out so they won't feel hurt
- feel like they have no other option, so they need to retreat

Turtles are all about feeling safe and protected. When things get rough, they prefer to wait it out by going internal and hiding within. You know you are dealing with a turtle if the individual suddenly becomes quiet and stops participating in the conversation. However, sometimes, retreating within is not enough, and if they feel pushed or attacked further, turtles might snap and bite the attacker. We call this a snapping turtle.

If you find yourself speaking with a turtle or a snapping turtle, remember that they need enough time and space to process the situation and feel safe. Give them time to adjust and process the information. Keep in mind the following:

- Turtles want to feel safe. Then they won't have to hide or snap.
- They need extra time to adjust to new situations or people.
- Their protective shell is very important. It lets them feel at home and safe.

When Speaking with Snapping Turtles

Sometimes, turtles feel like retreating is not enough, so they snap, cut you down, or bite.

Give them enough space to process the situation and let them feel safe to have the conversation.

If you notice yourself being a turtle or a snapping turtle, you can start by asking yourself, "Which of my needs is not being met?" Usually, it's the need for certainty, the need for love and connection, or the need for significance that requires attention in a turtle. Try to communicate this and ask the other person to reschedule this important conversation for when you feel more ready to discuss the issue at hand.

If you know you have a tendency to snap when pushed to a certain degree, start noticing your level of emotional irritation. If, for example, you know that you snap when your level of irritation reaches 10 on a scale of 0 to 10, you need to give others a warning at your irritation level of 6 or 7 so they know that they need to back off. Ask to reschedule the conversation until you have had time to think about it. This can be very useful when it comes to any relationship.

It really helps to know and understand these communication styles. I know, for example, that when my husband becomes a ram, I often turn into a turtle. However, knowing what the ram wants, I can choose to repeat back to him what he is trying to communicate to me. This way, he feels heard and does not need to keep pushing me. I can also give him a quick warning when I don't feel comfortable discussing the issue at hand in the given moment and ask to reschedule the conversation for another time. By then, I can be better mentally prepared to discuss it.

Prototype 4: The Dog

Dogs are ...

- loyal
- eager to be by your side no matter what
- willing to stick by you even when mistreated or misunderstood
- self-sacrificing
- unable to say no
- always wanting to help

The dog is the sweetest, kindest, most self-sacrificing, and loving of all four animal communication styles. A dog will do anything to make the other person happy. If you are a dog owner, just think of your dog for a second. When you feel sad, that dog comes to you and gives you a nudge to give you reassurance and support, just to make you feel a little better, as if saying, "Can I just be with you, do all I can for you, and give you everything I can?"

When I think of this prototype, I honestly think of my dear mom. Whenever I call her and ask, "Mom, can you please ..." she does not even wait for me to finish my sentence before responding with a resounding, "Yes I can. Anything for you!"

If You Are a Dog

You value kindness, love, and a sense of shared purpose. Think how to honor this part of yourself. Know that just being there sometimes is not enough. Sometimes you need to have a conversation or switch tactics.

I know many of us moms are dogs for our children. We would walk into a burning building for them. We would sacrifice anything for them. However, as much as we are willing to do practically everything we can for our kids, we need to keep in mind that being a dog does not always help them (or us).

The downside of being a dog is that it may enable others to continue behaviors that don't serve them, while possibly hurting them at the same time. So if you find yourself being a dog for someone, remember to honor this side of yourself, but also keep in mind the importance of healthy turtle boundaries, the persistence of a ram, and the relaxation of a grasshopper.

COACHING TIPS

- Think of your recent interaction with another person where you were a ram. How did you feel? What did the other person do? Did they become a turtle, a grasshopper, or a ram also? With the knowledge you have now, what would you have done differently?
- Think of a turtle, a grasshopper, and a ram you know and recall your last interaction with that person. Knowing what you know now, how would you approach the conversation differently? Make a note for yourself to do that next time.
- Think of a recent interaction with your child. Which animal communication style did your child use? Which one did you use? Knowing what you have just learned here, what could you have done differently? Plan to do that next time.

Elevate, Educate, Empower

Now that we know the importance of listening and the four animal communication styles, we must learn to allow our children to make their own choices. This is very important, because it is the subject of many arguments, especially with teenagers. I want you to be a true leader for your children: to inspire, not just manage, and to trust and empower them to make their own smart choices. If you don't, they might start making bad choices just to show you that they can.

Yes, trust takes courage, and I know you have it. That is why you are here, reading this book. So start showing your kids that you trust them. To illustrate this point, here is an example of a conversation between a mom and her sixteen-year-old daughter.

Mom: Where are you going?
Daughter (not looking at Mom): To a party.
Mom: Is there going to be alcohol at this party?
Daughter (with a smirk): I think so.
Mom: Are you going to drink?
Daughter (rolling her eyes): Um, probably.
Mom: Are you going to get in the car after that?
Daughter (scoffing): Maybe.

By the end of this conversation, Mom is going berserk, and the daughter thinks her mom is being ridiculous.

Now, let's try this conversation again, but this time we will hear what the daughter really wants to say (this is not what she's actually saying, because she doesn't want to get in trouble, but this is what she's thinking without saying it out loud). Here is this conversation again with the translations between the lines:

Mom: Where are you going?
Daughter: To a party. *[I know it's gonna bother you, since you don't trust me.]*
Mom: Is there going to be alcohol at this party?
Daughter: I think so. *[And if it bothers you, then definitely yes!]*
Mom: Are you going to drink?
Daughter: Um, probably. *[And if it bothers you a lot, I will drink a lot!]*
Mom: Are you going to get in the car after that?
Daughter: Maybe. *[Well, a ridiculous question deserves a ridiculous answer.]*

This is just a small illustration of how a child—in this case, a teenager—might act rebellious when they see that they are not being trusted.

This girl is smart. She does not have a death wish. She knows better, but sometimes when teenagers resent their parents not trusting them to make their own choices and their own decisions, they will make bad choices simply out of spite. They will do this just to prove to their parents that they have the power to make their own choices, even if those choices are not in alignment with what the parents want for them.

Here is what the mom in this scenario is doing: she is showing lack of trust in her daughter and pushing in such a way that it backfires. Instead, as the leaders of our households, we as parents must move our communication and parenting up to the next level. Which brings us to the true leader's EEE: elevate, educate, and empower.

If the mom in the conversation we just played-acted was a true leader and used the "elevate, educate, and empower" strategy, this conversation would probably have never taken place. If it did, it might sound somewhat like this recent conversation I had with my sixteen-year-old son:

Me: Hey! It's Friday. Any plans for tonight?
Sam: Oh, I got invited to a friend's party.
Me: How nice! Do you want a ride? How will you get there and back?
Sam: Um, I think I will just take Uber.
Me: That's smart. It may be safer, since there is probably going to be alcohol at the party.
Sam: There is, but I won't be drinking.
Me: That's cool. Just be safe and have a great time!
Sam: I'll be safe, don't worry.

At the end of this conversation, Sam felt that he was being trusted to make good choices, and I felt assured that he was going to be okay.

The First E: Elevate

I like this quote from Matthew Jacobson: "Behind every young child who believes in himself is a parent who believed first." With that said, I want you to start elevating your child. Remember, we started doing that in the STARS strategy earlier when we talked about the five elements of building a fantastic relationship with your child. If you forgot, please go back to it and review that strategy in Step 2 chapter.

Elevation is so important. It enables our children to believe in themselves. I want you to start seeing the good in your child. Praise, compliment, and thank your kids for every good thing that they do, whether it's for you, for others, or even for themselves. Keep telling them how proud you are of them. That elevates and empowers your child.

Elevation is the first and very important thing that you must start with. Just start complimenting, thanking, and telling your children how lucky you are to be their mom or dad.

Teach Empowerment by believing in their power. The best way to teach kids about how great they are is to convince yourself of it first. I want you to start seeing your child as a wonderful, extraordinary person. I want you to start seeing all the good that's there. If you believe in your child's power and greatness, then every interaction will confirm it. Just watch and see.

A few years ago, I took my kids on a vacation trip to Mexico—just the three of us. Abi was twelve and Sam was ten. That's when, for the first time, I discovered how musical my daughter really was, which I didn't realize before. Abi could listen to a song and break it up into all the separate voices and instruments. She could separate out each instrument's voice from the rest and sing what each instrument was playing. I was amazed at that, and I had to express it and tell her how proud I was of her. I knew she was very musical but didn't realize she was that good.

So say it. When you notice something good in your kid, say it out loud. As mentioned before, it's not possible to overcompliment someone, even your child. Every compliment you pay is an investment in your child's emotional bank account and your relationship.

The Second E: Educate

When focusing on the *education* part of the true leader's EEE, focus on teaching, not preaching. Teach through stories, not rules. Share your thoughts and opinions, and ask for your child's as well. Let this be a dialogue.

Don't be afraid to show your vulnerability or share your feelings, including fears. Casual conversation that starts with elevation, the first E, is the best way to relax kids enough so they become open and ready to hear what you want to say. Have an open discussion and let your child learn by asking questions.

Unfortunately, many kids understand from a very young age that adults teach rules, requirements, and laws. They are all about "Warning," "Caution," "Stop," and "Danger!" Adults tell kids what they should do, what they shouldn't do, what they must do, what they mustn't do, and so on.

I've got news for you: these are all turnoffs for kids. These pull kids away from alignment with their Inner Being. We talked about how important that alignment is. After a while, as they keep interacting with us, our kids might start to tune us (adults) out.

So what do most parents do? Well, they get louder, of course!

The truth is, it doesn't work, because kids, if they weren't afraid to get in trouble for saying this, would tell us, "Yeah, I heard you. I just don't believe you." If they could really articulate this, they would say, "You're telling me what to do and not to do, but I'm standing here in fun and freedom and eagerness about life, and I don't think I want to follow your path."

Okay, so the simple fact is that most parents (and they don't mean to do this, by the way) focus attention away from alignment. They do it with their demands, commands, and worries. But what they're doing is trying to help their children "be right in the world" and present themselves in such a way that the parents will be proud of them.

Most kids will try to comply for a while, and they will play that game with us parents. They will do as we tell them, and they will go along with our demands and commands. But after the first few years, and especially when they get into the preteen years, they begin to figure this out, and that's when we start having communication issues.

The thing about neurodiverse kids, such as those with ADHD, is that they cannot comply to begin with. They are naturally noncompliant. They come into this world with a choice made by their inner being prior to their physical birth that they would not be able to comply and conform to others' expectations. This way, they could simply focus on creating their own reality, their own world.

If you believe that we make a choice of the path we will take before we enter into this physical realm, then you will also believe that neurodiverse people (such as those with ADHD, ODD, and autism) have made the choice to be that way with a simple purpose: to have no distractions from creating their own reality. They are noncompliant from the start so they will not have to bend to the rules of others or fit into someone's framework or box.

Talk to your kids when they are ready to hear you. You will know when they are—they will act receptive. They will act open and want to talk. They will actually show you that they want to hear what you have to say. However, I have to warn you: you cannot teach something to someone who is not asking for it.

I heard this joke once: What is the one commodity where the supply always exceeds the demand? The answer is unsolicited advice. The truth is, we don't like it when others give us unsolicited advice, so why do we think it's okay to do it to our kids?

Again, you cannot teach something to someone who is not asking for it. Yes, you can go through the motions, you can make kids jump through hoops, you can get them to say back to you like a parrot whatever you said, but it's pointless. Words don't teach. It's the experience that teaches.

My parents, my kids' grandparents, often complain that they're trying to teach Abi by telling her the mistakes to avoid, but she still makes those mistakes. This is a perfect illustration of the point that words don't teach, especially when it comes to ADHD children.

Remember, since we all create our own reality, life experience comes from *creating* that experience. This is why it's so hard to teach kids with ADHD—they just don't want to hear you. They want to create their own experience and learn from that.

Our life experiences come from what we want to attract into our reality. So to help children create a sense of well-being, soothe them into the expectation of that well-being. That's the most and the best we can do for them. When we soothe them into expecting good—expecting well-being—this puts them in the place of receiving that well-being, receiving inspiration, so that they can create their own beautiful reality.

Remember, we are the happiest when we create. Let your children create their own experiences while you create yours. Let inspiration be your guide, because when we feel inspired, we are connected to source energy, to infinite intelligence.

Inspiration Is Connection to Infinite Intelligence

Infinite intelligence is where great composers get their ideas for beautiful music. This is where artists, writers, and poets get information for their next masterpiece. This is where scientists receive breakthrough ideas. All they need to do is plug into infinite intelligence. We call that state of mind the feeling of being plugged into the infinite intelligence inspiration.

So get inspired. Let inspiration be your guide. And when you do, ride that wave of inspiration as long as you can to make the most of your human experience and create the most wonderful, amazing reality for yourself and your loved ones.

How do you get inspiration? You get aligned first. Inspiration comes from being in touch with your inner being—only then you can tap into source energy and creativity.

Let your children get inspired so they can use that inspiration to create their own fantastic experience for themselves. This means teaching them alignment by your own example.

ADHD kids, and ADHD adults too, want to create their own reality; they learn from that the best, so let them. Do not teach processes; teach by being. Be aligned with yourself, and then your children will gravitate toward you. It's much more effective than "Do as I say, not as I do." When your children gravitate toward you because you are aligned, they will want to learn from you. They will want to know, "Why are you so happy? Why aren't you like most other adults? I want to be like you."

Do not teach processes. Teach by being. Teach kids to get in alignment with their own true self, their inner being, by demonstrating your own alignment with your inner being. This means you must be in alignment with your inner being first. You must be in thriving mode.

The Third E: Empower

Empower your kids by believing in their own power first. Believe that all the goodness and love you have invested in them so far is there to guide them. Elevating and empowering your children on a daily basis, saying how much you believe in them, is the greatest investment you can make in their happy and healthy future.

Empower them to make wise choices. As we discussed, absolutely do talk about the circumstances and consequences of their potential actions— what could possibly happen before and after they do what they want to do. But then, ultimately, let them learn to make their own choices.

If you listen to *The Teachings of Abraham* by Esther and Jerry Hicks, you will hear that if you make the choices for your children and expect them to listen and do as they're told, they will only learn to please and obey you. That's not what you *really* want, though.

Ultimately, our children need to learn to make good healthy choices on their own, and we must believe in our children's ability to make those good choices.

As a true leader, you want to first give your children roots and then wings. You have probably heard that expression before. What you can do for your children is give them roots—meaning a foundation of good education, strong ethical and moral values, and family traditions. You have probably been doing that since their birth. However, then you must let them go. Give them wings to have the freedom to make their own choices.

Empower them to use that freedom to make choices, and trust that they are capable of making choices for themselves. Again, trust takes courage, which you must demonstrate. Because you're a leader, you must show courage.

To wrap up this chapter, I have this quote for you from Ann Landers: "It's not what you do for your children, but what you have taught them to do for themselves, that will make them successful human beings." Go on and be a great leader for your family and a true leader of your life.

Key Points

- It's time for you to become a true leader of your family.
- Being a true leader means knowing how to listen and communicate effectively and how to respond in a calm, constructive manner rather than reacting emotionally.
- You must lead by inspiring and uplifting, rather than managing and punishing.
- The four animal communication styles offer a useful strategy for improving communication with anyone. Remember, with rams, you need to repeat back to them what they are telling you. With grasshoppers, speak in a cheerful way, or join them in their activity while talking. With turtles, make them feel safe, give them time, and let them come to you.
- Empower your children to make their own choices. You want them to grow up independent and capable of making decisions for themselves. You cannot make decisions for them forever, so start now: give them roots and then wings.
- Remember the true leader's EEE: elevate, educate, and empower. Elevate and praise your children constantly for what is already working. Educate your children, but only when they are open to listening. Teach by being. Empower your children by believing in their power first.

Summary and Conclusion

Imagine who you want your kids to become, then be that.
—*Author Unknown*

Wow! Can you believe this? We are now in the concluding chapter of this book, *From Havoc to Harmony: Five Steps to Restore Peace at Home and Rebuild Your Relationship with Your ADHD Child.* By now, you should be very familiar with these five steps, and here we will simply summarize and wrap up.

The Five Steps

Step 1: Reframe the Situation

In step 1 (chapter 1), we talked about the importance of reframing the situation—and specifically reframing how we view ADHD from being a disorder to being a neurodiversity. Your child is not disabled, just different. By now, I hope, you have been able to shift your focus away from what is not working and how your ADHD child simply cannot fit into the old framework set up by older generations and structures, such as school systems.

Those approaches don't work anymore, at least not for our ADHD kids. Instead, focus on what is good: this amazing, brilliant, creative human being you have in your life. Think of the many important lessons your child is teaching you right now—lessons like how to be patient, understanding, loving, accepting, and so much more.

We talked about the fact that ADHD people are actually quite valuable, and we named many talented brilliant individuals through history up until the modern day—the geniuses and legends with ADHD, people like Michael Jordan, Vincent van Gogh, Mozart, and Leonardo da Vinci.

Then we talked about the advantages of ADHD, how ADHD people are such valuable members of our society, how we actually need those people, how their minds work faster than others', and how they are more resilient, creative, and passionate. What we need to do is learn to embrace this neurodiversity. We really can have ADHD people rock our world and make a difference if we just embrace that.

Then we touched a little bit on brain anatomy and physiology; the structures and the functions of an ordinary brain versus an ADHD brain; and how in the ADHD brain, the filter between emotions and responses is not as strong as in an ordinary brain. That is what makes an ADHD brain more prone to meltdowns and sometimes aggressive outbursts, but it also makes it more brilliant, creative, and amazing in many ways.

Speaking of aggressive behaviors, we discussed the teenage brain and how it's wired for survival—specifically, how aggressive behavior is an evolutionary tool for selection of the fittest and the strongest, and how brain chemistry is set for aggressive behavior around the teenage years, when individuals are meant to climb the social scale to establish themselves. More aggressive individuals rose to become leaders. Nowadays, around puberty, at the ages of fourteen, fifteen, and sixteen, kids are still in school. But thousands or even just a few hundred years ago, people at these ages were considered adults.

Then we talked about dealing with difficult and aggressive behaviors. We discussed how you can deal with those behaviors of your child and how to work through conflicts. We talked about the importance of recognizing whether your child's aggression also brings out aggression in you. We introduced the importance of addressing your well-being and your inner alignment with yourself before you can effectively communicate with your child—or anyone, for that matter.

Remember, do not interact with your child when you are frustrated, angry, or disappointed, because in that state, at that moment, you're not in alignment with yourself. When you are not in alignment, you cannot be an effective parent. When you are in alignment (and you know when you are in alignment because it feels good to you emotionally), you come from a place of love, kindness, and joy, and you make a greater impact on your child. So it's all about alignment.

Step 2: Understand Your Child's Needs

In step 2 (chapter 2), we talked about understanding your child's needs and how you must really listen to do that. We went over the six human needs and the healthy and unhealthy ways that people meet those needs. These six needs are:

1. Certainty
2. Variety
3. Love and connection
4. Significance
5. Growth
6. Contribution

These are the basic six needs that we all want to have met, and if those needs are not met, we feel unfulfilled, unhappy, or in other words, misaligned. So basically, we are not thriving when our needs are not met. Our kids are not thriving and not aligned when their needs are not met.

We talked about paying special attention to three of the needs: certainty, significance, and love and connection. These are really big in the world of our kids these days, especially teens and preteens. We talked about how if your kids don't get those needs met at home, they will look elsewhere. They will go online for that connection (to feel like they belong) or on social media to feel significant (feel important and special). They will start engaging in behaviors that might not be healthy or safe for them. We want to make sure to give them that sense of certainty, love/connection, and significance at home, and we talked about different ways you can do that, starting today.

When our needs are not met, our expectations are not met. We feel loss, and the sense of loss feels painful. The result of that sense of loss and pain usually is anger or sadness. So to help avoid or prevent these in our kids, to help them meet their needs, we introduced the STARS (smile, thank, align, respect, show), which I hope you are now practicing every day.

Remember, in the STARS, S is for *smile* when you see them or greet them and be fully present for them for the full sixty seconds. *T* is for *thanks*, which reminds you to focus on appreciating them. Compliment and thank them every day. *A* is for your *alignment*, which means you need to be authentically aligned with yourself and let go of what you don't like, including complaining about what you don't want. Remember, when we complain about something, we focus on it, and therefore, we attract more of it. *R* is for *respect*, which means always being polite and respectful. Stop arguing. And the last *S* is for *showing* kids affection through physical expression, such as hugs, kisses, pats on the back, or any way they feel comfortable accepting.

Finally, use your words to communicate to your child how important it is for you to be the best parent you can be. I know that you are already doing your best, because you are reading this book. So have your mom or dad mission statement and communicate that to your child.

As we concluded the discussion of our children's needs, we mentioned that their needs do not include meeting our needs, which means that we must meet our own needs. It's our responsibility.

Step 3: Meet Your Needs

Remember, it's common for parents to struggle in shifting to meet their own needs. There's nothing wrong with meeting your needs. If you feel guilty, you are not alone. I want you to know that. However, I'm going to use the words of Dr. Ellen Kreidman, the relationship expert from whom I took my first relationship course. She said, "Feel guilty and do it anyway." Because your feeling guilty is better (for your loved ones) than your feeling angry or sad.

So remember: if your needs are not met (and you have the same six human needs), you feel upset, frustrated, stressed, or unhappy. However, it's your responsibility, not your child's responsibility, to make you happy and meet your needs.

We talked about the wheel of wellness and how all the dimensions of this wheel are interconnected. When one dimension is compromised, the rest follow. This means that you must maintain all these dimensions in good health, in good standing. And you start with the intellectual dimension of the wheel of wellness: your mind.

You have probably heard about this mind-over-body phenomenon. Now think of the next level: mind over everything, not just mind over body. Your mind over everything!

I told you the story of the man and his Tree of Livelihood and how taking care of the leaves is not as effective as watering the roots of this tree. So what are the roots of *your* Tree of Livelihood? That's your mind-set. The root of your Tree of Livelihood, the root of your well-being, is your alignment with your inner being. It's the core of who you really are—the part of you that wants to thrive; wants love; wants harmony, peace, and good. This is why you start with the intellectual dimension, the mind, on that wheel of wellness, because the right mind-set can shift everything in your life for the better.

When we are not in the right mind-set, when we are misaligned, we are not thriving. Instead, we are in the surviving mode of being, which limits our own creativity, our field of vision, and our ability to receive inspiration. When we're in thriving mode, we can get inspired, tap into the infinite intelligence, and connect with source energy. We can get creative ideas, and we can solve our problems in ways that we could not see before when we were limited by the surviving mode.

So whatever you do, wherever you are, I ask you to make a decision to be happy no matter what. Because, remember, happiness is a choice. It depends only on you. You can choose to be happy or not. I want you to shift your mode of being from surviving into thriving, and to do that you need to rewire your brain to establish new patterns in your thought processes.

We talked about how, in order to shift into thriving mode, you need to rewire your brain by practicing new thought patterns on a regular basis. I want you to think of this as a daily exercise, like going to the gym. It's like a workout for your brain: training your brain and practicing these simple steps on a regular basis. That's where we introduced the BOSS (breathe, observe, stretch, and self-affirmation) strategy so you can reclaim power over your own life and be the boss of your thoughts, emotions, and life.

Here's your exercise routine that I gave you specifically to practice the

BOSS. At least two or three times a day (or you can do it more frequently), you must pretend (for practice sake) to have a negative emotion or your trigger (negative thought or interaction). Then you go through the BOSS steps:

- Take a deep *breath.*
- *Observe* yourself and your surroundings.
- *Stretch.*
- Repeat your *self-affirmation* statement.

By taking a deep breath and observing yourself and your surroundings, you put yourself into the present moment. By taking a stretch as you say in your mind your self-affirmation statement, you anchor the positive thought with emotion to the shift in your physical state. (Note: Some people, instead of the stretch, prefer to anchor the positive feeling through a small movement, such as putting their hand on their chest or touching a ring on their hand. Find what small physical gesture works for you as an anchor move.)

Remember your self-affirmation (or your power) statement as you do the anchor move every time. This needs to be a short but easy-to-remember statement you can quickly say in your mind multiple times a day. There is an optional additional component, which is to visualize yourself in that elevated state. For those people who are visual, it helps to picture themselves in an empowered position, feeling strong, confident, and happy. If you are a visual person, hold that image in your mind while you are doing the stretch and saying your self-affirmation statement.

This exercise is extremely effective in helping rewire the brain. I have applied it with my coaching clients many times, and it does wonders for them. As the brain gets rewired for thriving, it becomes easier and easier to respond positively, even in situations that seem negative.

This is a gradual process; it won't happen overnight. And honestly, I'm still working on mine every so often. But once you have your brain rewired into thriving, your whole life can gradually change for the better, and you can make positive responses and interact with your child and others in a positive way.

Step 4: Respond, Not React

In this chapter, the discussion was about becoming an effective communicator. We talked about the difference between reacting versus responding to people and situations, and how in many interactions with others, we expect them to change their behavior so that we can feel better, or they expect us to change our behavior so that they can feel better. This is a common cause of arguments, disappointment, and frustration on either or both sides of the interaction.

We talked about how this type of interaction does not really work for anyone because no one can make other people feel alignment with their inner being if they do not feel it on the inside. This means that you cannot make another person, such as your child, feel aligned, and your child cannot make you feel aligned. This is each person's own responsibility.

We talked about how it's up to you to make the decision that you're going to feel good no matter how your child behaves. Once you've made that decision, using positive responses to even negative events can lead to positive outcomes. I gave you specific tips of what to do and say in situations that you may perceive as negative.

Remember, when you find yourself in a situation when you feel upset (in other words, misaligned), I want you to stop and ask yourself two very important questions: *Which one of my six human needs is not being met?* and then, once you've identified which one of those six needs is not met, *What do I really want in this moment?* After you've identified which of the six needs must be met and what you really want, you can figure out how else you can meet that need. Think creatively and figure out alternative ways to meet that need for yourself.

We then talked about what you can do as an effective communicator when your child (or another person you are interacting with) is feeling upset, and how you can respond effectively instead of reacting. When emotions are high, people cannot be receptive. So when your child (or someone else) is feeling upset or misaligned, it's useless to try to reason with them, try to convince them of something, or plead. What you must do first is stop arguing. You simply avoid engaging in the arguing behavior, the banter, the back and forth. Instead, you say, "I understand. What can I do to make you feel better?"

Remember, when kids are emotional, they cannot be reasoned with, so it's better to have a rational conversation after they have cooled down. When they're emotional, they cannot be rational. Just remember that very simple truth, and in the meantime, this is what you can say: "Okay, I understand. What can I do to make you feel better?" Bottom line, when your focus is in the right place, which is your own alignment, you are more likely to respond instead of reacting.

Here's another thing that I want you to write down and have as part of your daily routine of what you say to yourself, like a mantra: Love and accept yourself just the way you are, and then love and accept your children just the way they are. I know this is not simple or easy, and it takes practice, and it takes rewiring your brain by practicing the new way of thinking, but that's the only way to find harmony within and without.

So let yourself be yourself and let them be themselves. I hope by now you have written this somewhere so you can look at it every day to remind you to let yourself be yourself. You are perfect the way you are, and they are perfect the way they are. Period.

Step 5: Become a True Leader

Once you have practiced accepting yourself and accepting your child, being in thriving mode, and being an effective communicator, now you're ready to become a true leader. In Chapter 5, we talked about what that means.

There are three great attributes of true leaders. First of all, true leaders really listen; and only after listening do they speak. We learned that from Nelson Mandela.

Second, true leaders lead by example, instead of managing. How many times have you heard, "Do as I say, not as I do"? Unfortunately, it's just too common. It's funny but at the same time sad that so many people try to manage by telling others what to do instead of leading by example. I want you to start leading by example—the example of alignment. If you are in alignment yourself, that will teach your child to also find alignment within.

Third, true leaders inspire. They inspire, elevate, and allow others to be themselves and be the greatest, best versions of themselves that they can be. We talked about how you need to empower your child by believing in your child's power; that in turn will empower your kid to learn to make choices. If you make all the choices for your children, they will learn only to mind you, only to please you. They need to learn to make good choices on their own. So you must believe in your children's ability to make good choices, then elevate and praise them for making those good choices.

So what you can do for your children is give them roots: the foundation of good education, strong moral values, and family traditions. Then you let them go and give them wings: the freedom to create their own reality. I know this takes trust, and trust takes courage—a lot of courage. I know, and I believe that you have it. If you are reading this book, I believe you have that courage.

We concluded the chapter with a true leader's EEE:

- **Elevate** your child by practicing the STARS strategy every day.
- **Educate** by example of your own alignment and practice your alignment by practicing the four Ps strategy every day.
- **Empower** your children by believing in their ability, and inspire them to be great, to be the best human beings they can be.

It's Your Time!

I have been here to elevate, educate, and empower *you*. It's your time; it's the time for you to take control. Become a true leader in your home and your life—not an angry, frustrated parent dealing with a resentful kid but a true leader of your family in every sense of the word.

Teach well-being by being happy. If you get nothing else out of this book except this simple truth, I would say my mission is accomplished. I want you to teach your child well-being by being happy yourself. It's all about your relationship with yourself. When that is good, everything else falls into place. That's the bottom line.

Be playful about it. The happier you are, the more your children will listen to you. The more aligned you are, the better you will feel to your children. Remember: they are already aligned, because they have come into this world aligned. And because they came into this world more recently than you, they are more aligned than you. So the better you feel to them, the more they will gravitate toward you.

> - Have fun with it!
> - Be playful about it.
> - Let your behavior and attitude speak for you.
> - The happier you are, the more your child will listen to you.
> - The more aligned you are, the better you will feel to your child.
> - The better you feel to your child, the more your child will gravitate toward you.

We all come into this world aligned from birth. We become misaligned later, when others (including parents, grandparents, teachers, and other well-meaning folks) start telling us that there is something wrong with us. They try to change our behavior so they can feel better. How often do we say to our kids, when we get frustrated with them, "What's wrong with you?!" How often have you heard that same phrase from your parents and teachers? Hearing this makes us believe that there is something wrong with us indeed, which puts us immediately out of alignment. It's disempowering.

Then, as we grow up, we get pushed out of alignment with all the rules and regulations of what we should and should not do. Our society, our parents, and our schools do that to us, and this is why kids don't get what most adults try to say. They don't get it because most adults are not aligned.

You see, kids haven't been around that long. They came into this world much more recently than us, so they are more aligned. If you want to be closer to your kids, just be authentically aligned, because most kids are already naturally aligned. Get into alignment because then and only then will you be closer to your child, who is already in alignment.

Be playful! Teach your kids to get in alignment with their own true self, their inner being. The only way to teach this is by demonstrating your own alignment with your inner being. This means that you must be in alignment with your inner being first, and you must be in thriving mode in order to be in alignment. Your alignment and thriving go hand and hand.

The farewell quote I want you to take with you today is this: "Parenting isn't a practice. It's a daily learning experience."

Parenting is a process. It's a journey, not a destination. You're not going to be done when your kids are eighteen. You're not going to be done when they get married or finish college. It's a never-ending experience. It's an ongoing learning experience, ever-changing and evolving. So make the most out of it. Have fun with it and enjoy this ride, even if at times it feels like a crazy roller coaster. Get adventurous, and you will see how much you have to gain and how your relationship with your spirited child or teen grows, expands, and flourishes as a result.

If I could go back to my old self on that sad afternoon when Abi blurted out to then-desperate me, "It's your problem, not mine," I would tell myself: *You know, she is actually right. This is not your child's problem. The way you are looking at this situation is the real problem.*

Once I stopped focusing on "the problem" and started focusing on appreciating my daughter for the wonderful human being she really is, our whole relationship dynamic shifted. I no longer see her ADHD or her behavior as a problem. She is unique and amazing in her own way, bright and beautiful, and I am so proud of the young woman she is becoming.

This is Abi on her prom night: a happy and healthy young lady who is confident, independent, and strong.

I stumbled on this quote the other day: "A daughter is just a little girl who grows up to be your best friend." This could not be truer, but I was the one who had to grow up to fully understand this and let it happen. Achieving peace at home and shifting from havoc to harmony in your relationship is possible. And if I could do this with my ADHD kid, I know you can too.

I hope, my story will inspire you, or at least show you that you can create a beautiful relationship with your spirited ADHD child or teen. Now you have all these useful tools and strategies to help you on the way.

Now I want to hear your stories. Write to me and share. I can't wait to hear from you.

Appendix:
Bonus Chapters

༄༅ ༜

Sibling Rivalry

ༀ

"I swear, I will stop the car if you two don't stop this right now!" she yells while glaring in the rearview mirror as her four-year-old and six-year-old scream at each other in the back seat. They are fighting again. Over something silly. Again.

Ignoring their mom's warnings and angry looks, they keep going.

"Stop! Give it back!"

"No, you stop! Get away from me!"

"Mom, tell him!"

"That's it!" she snaps. "I've had enough. I am pulling over!" With her insides boiling in rage, she pulls out of traffic to stop the car on the shoulder of the freeway, trying to collect herself before addressing the children again. "This needs to stop, kids! What is going on now? Why can't you just get along?"

Sound familiar? If you said yes, then you are one of many parents dealing with sibling rivalry on a daily basis.

Why Do They Fight?

Where is all the fighting coming from? Most of the time, we get upset when our needs or expectations are not met. When our needs are not met, we feel a sense of loss, which leads to pain, and emotional pain usually manifests itself in anger or sadness. The same goes for our children, no matter how young they are.

Even when you try your best to help your kids meet their needs, they still may feel frustrated by their brother or sister when they experience one or more of the following:

- **Need for space:** One sibling wants to be left alone, while the other wants to interact.
- **Unmet expectations:** Just as unmet needs lead to pain and anger, unmet expectations lead to sense of loss, which leads in turn to a sense of pain and anger or frustration.

- **Different developmental stages**: Children of different ages will have different needs from each other.
- **Competition**: Kids may sense unequal treatment either at home or outside of home.
- **Need for attention**: When kids do not receive positive attention from parents, they will try to get any attention, including negative attention.

Sometimes, it's all of the above. And when the pent-up frustration reaches the limit, children seek the safest person to let this frustration out on. Unfortunately, in many cases, a brother or sister seems like the safest person for that. After all, a sibling (especially a younger one) can't punish the way parents can.

With all that said, I want to add that some level of sibling rivalry is actually normal and will probably always be there. It does not mean that you as a parent are doing anything wrong. It is simply part of human nature, and it's acceptable.

My sister and I are about four and a half years apart, and until our teenage years, we were fighting quite a lot, in spite of playing together all through our childhood. I am the older sister, and I have always felt the need to take care of her when our parents were not around. She, as the younger one, has always looked up to me (or so she tells me). Now that we are adults and have become mothers ourselves, we chat about those times, and she tells me that all she wanted was to be just like me. I find that endearing and sweet, because I have always felt quite maternal toward her.

In spite of these feelings of affection toward each other, we would still get into bickering spells as children. We no longer fight because of the distance and the limited time we get to spend with each other—we each have a family with children of our own—but if we were stuck together for more than a week, we would probably find something to argue about. What I am trying to say is that siblings, no matter how much they love each other (and they do!), will always find something to fight about. It's normal.

My kids, Abi and Sam, used to fight over the smallest things, but I know they love each other and care for each other deeply. As an example, one time I was picking up the kids from school, and Sam, seven at the time, was already in the car. Abi, nine years old, was taking forever, as usual. She had not been diagnosed with ADHD at that time, so I could not understand why it was taking her so long to pack her backpack and get out of the classroom. She was always the last student to leave the class.

After twenty minutes of waiting, I blurted out in frustration, "That's it. I've had it! We are leaving without Abi."

To my surprise, Sam got very vocal in protesting that we could not just leave Abi at school. That's when he stood up for his sister for the first time.

How sweet! I thought. *He must really care about his sister.* I understood then how much he actually loved her in spite of all the fighting and bickering at home.

That was an interesting observation I made that day—one of many discoveries I made as part of my parenting journey. However, I wish there was someone who could have taught me what I am about to share with you here.

Common Parenting Mistakes

I did not realize I was making some common mistakes with my children that can actually promote the rivalry between them. Now I know better, and I am sharing them with you. What are these common mistakes?

1. **Being all-inclusive all the time:** Parents often try to make sure that no one is left out, but that's not really necessary. Particularly if the children are different either developmentally or temperamentally, this does not work. Activities (including fun activities, like games) must be appropriate for each child individually. So making both kids do the same thing at the same time may cause frustration and resentment between them.

2. **Creating competition:** Even when you think it's a healthy competition, such as "Let's see who can get dressed faster" or "Let's see who can be quieter," this creates resentment between the loser and the winner in this game. Children need to be praised for their own individual achievements. The bar needs to be set just right for each child to be challenged a little but not too much that it becomes a put-down. Basically, each child needs to have

an individual progress chart. Always compare children to their yesterday-self, so to speak.

3. **Labeling or creating a superstar**: When one of the siblings gets labeled as the star of the family, the other sibling feels left out or inadequate. This is very similar to creating a competition, except the left-out child feels unable to compete. Both children must feel special in their own way. Review the six human needs—each person, no matter how young, has a need for love and connection and a need for significance. Parents must help children meet those needs and teach them how to meet those needs for themselves.

What You Can Do

If you are caught in the middle of a bickering session between your kids, there are several things you can do to interrupt the pattern on the spot:

1. **Switch the current activity.** Whatever the kids are busy fighting about, give them something different to do. Occupy their attention with a different activity or interest. Give them a new assignment or ask them for help, or simply give them a new game to play. If you can participate in that new game, that's even better!

2. **Change the scenery.** Move from inside to outside, from outside to inside, or simply from one room to another. There is a phenomenon called the *threshold effect*. Many people don't realize it, but when we walk through a door threshold, our brain switches, like turning a page in a book. You know how sometimes you go to a different room and forget what you came for, so you go back to the previous room to remember what it was that you forgot? That's the threshold effect, and you can use it to your advantage to switch the attention of the fighting siblings.

3. **Let them figure it out.** Sometimes, you just need to give them a chance to work it out on their own. In some cases, kids can work out their differences without an adult getting involved, especially if they were taught to use words to communicate their needs to others. If they cannot resolve their disagreement on their own,

you may need to step in and switch the topic, switch the activity, switch the scenery, or change the game.

What Not to Do

What does not work?

1. Punishing, timeouts, and/or taking things away does not work for ADHD kids or kids with neurodiversity. We have tried this with Abi, but all it did was make her more angry and frustrated in the long run. It also made her more resentful toward us, her parents, and her brother. At other times, taking away a toy did not work simply because Abi would switch her attention to something else. ADHD kids are actually more resilient in a way because they do not dwell on the negative too long.

2. Getting triggered by kids' fighting does not work, although it is so common among parents, especially when they are running on a low battery already. When we are physically exhausted (which is very common for parents of young children), our emotional tolerance tends to run low too. This is when it's important to make sure to address your own needs. If the kids' aggression toward each other brings out the aggression in you, this is a sign that your own needs are not being met, and you have to tend to them. It's okay to take care of yourself. If you don't do it, no one else will. If you notice that your kids' fighting triggers you to get frustrated or angry, stop and ask yourself: Which of my needs are not met? What do I really need now? When your own needs are met, you are more likely to stay calm and peaceful, even in a storm.

3. Taking sides or staying neutral can be tricky. This really depends on each individual situation, so you must use your best judgment. Never taking sides definitely does not work, nor does always taking a side. Yes, you must listen to both sides and hear them out, but each child feels sure of being in the right. And both children are, in their own way, because all they are trying to do is meet their own needs. Once again, it all comes down to helping both kids

meet their needs without hurting their sibling's feelings. Sounds simple, but it's not easy.

Preventing Sibling Fights

The best approach to the whole sibling rivalry issue is to prevent the outbursts and fights in the first place, as much as possible. As we discussed earlier, children, just like adults, get frustrated when their needs are not met. In most cases, the need for certainty, the need for love and connection, and the need for significance are the ones that require the most attention for children. They need to feel certain that their parents are always going to be there for them and that there is stability and routine in their lives. They need to feel that they are loved and taken care of. They need to feel important, appreciated, and special in their own unique way.

Oftentimes, jealousy, competition, or disruption of routine by a sibling's presence can trigger a feeling of loss and pain from an unmet need or expectation. There are two things you can do to make sure that your children feel that these needs are met: spend time with each child individually and unite your children by giving them a project to do together.

Spend Time with Each Child

Schedule some special time together with each of your children and keep it consistent, so they can count on this special time with you. This way, your child will feel important, loved, and connected to you.

For example, when my son Sam was younger, every Saturday after his piano lesson, I would take him to Amici's Pizza. I would let him order whatever he wanted, and while we waited for our pizzas, we played a game of Battleship. Sam and I still remember those fun times, as we felt very connected during that hour. It was just him and me, and that was our special time together.

I did something similar with Abi. We went to get our nails done together—that was our special "girl time" when it was just the two of us. Sam was not around, and we could connect on a deeper level as we talked about anything and everything.

See what your children love to do and do that with them. Think of what they enjoy doing individually and with you. Set aside time with each of them and schedule these regular appointments that both you and they can look forward to.

During your special time, make sure to thank and compliment each child. Make that child feel special and interesting. Be genuinely curious about that child's opinions and thoughts. You may be surprised by how much you can learn when you just let your child open up to your curiosity. When your children know that they are getting individual special attention from you, they won't need to fight each other for it.

Unite Your Children

Unite your children by giving them a project they can do together. Nothing connects people better than a common purpose. Just make sure that your children won't fight over who will do which part of the project, as that would just defeat the purpose. Let them decide how to get it done, and let them divide the tasks.

For example, you can have them grow a garden (or a small part of it) together. You can have them paint a room, take care of a pet, or decorate a Christmas tree. Let them make you breakfast or take care of you in some way (this is very effective!). Choose a project that is creative and fun and requires each of the kids to employ their individual special talents and skills while using creative ideas. Then praise, praise, and praise them some more for working well together, for being creative, and for finishing the project (or whatever it was).

Whichever methods you choose, you want to use positive attention (praise, thanks, and compliments). This will make wonderful deposits into their emotional bank accounts and will reduce the need for them to seek attention from you via fighting, jealous tantrums, or misbehaving. These three are ways to get negative attention from you because negative attention is better than no attention.

Therefore, make sure to give your kids lots of positive attention. Catch them in the act of being good and say it! Remember to always be polite with your children. Treat them with respect and appreciation, and most importantly, model for them by being happy and loving yourself.

Show them by feeling joy and peace yourself. This is the best way to teach your children peace, love, and harmony with each other and with the world.

Now, let me hear your stories. Write to me at coachgelena.com.

Your Child and Electronics

The whole topic of children and electronics is quite vast, and there is a lot of material out there, including all kinds of videos, articles, and blogs on various social media platforms. According to statistical research, most boys use electronics for video games, while most girls use electronics for social media. However, both boys and girls spend quite a considerable amount of time on both—social media and video games.

Social Media

Frankly, as I observe my own two teenagers, I can see that my son, age sixteen, spends quite a bit of time on video games, Snapchat for group messaging, and FaceTime for one-on-one calls. Meanwhile, my daughter, age eighteen, uses mostly Instagram, a little Snapchat, texting, and sometimes I see her FaceTime-ing her best friend (especially when they are deciding what to wear). Both kids use YouTube a lot. I have to admit, I use YouTube quite often too. Interestingly, Facebook and Twitter are not as popular with our kids as these other platforms.

According to Pew Research Center, at least 95 percent of teenagers have access to social media through their smartphones, and almost half of them say that they are online almost constantly. According to the latest statistics reports, YouTube, Snapchat, and Instagram are the top most used online platforms.

When asked about how they view social media, about a third of the interviewed teenagers feel that it's beneficial because it helps them stay connected with others, find information, and learn new things. About a fifth of the interviewed teenagers feel that social media has a negative impact because of cyberbullying, distraction, peer pressure, and emotional drama. The rest choose to stay neutral.

Considering that over 95 percent of teens use their smartphones for social media, it's needless to say that there has been a growing concern among parents about the influence of social media on our children. Parents are worried (and rightfully so) about their children being exposed to cyberstalking and cyberbullying or getting involved in dangerous behavior, such as sexting or posting inappropriate pictures online.

This is where it's important to remember that we cannot love our children and worry about them at the same time. Worrying is, by default, a type of conditional being and conditional living. When we worry about our children, we are basically saying to them, "I want you to change your behavior so that I can feel better." This does not work for us parents, and it does not work for our kids.

Keep in mind, our children came into this reality with a plan to create. They chose to come into this physical world at this particular time, where they would be on the leading edge of creation and all that comes with it, including today's technology. If you think that all the technological advancements and all the newly developed gadgets cause our children to get addicted to them, you've got it backward. The cause-and-effect relationship here is such that these technologies became manifested when the new generation of humans desired them; and for our children, it starts from a very young age.

Our children came into this world cable-ready. They came plugged in from birth. When we try to stop them from exploring and experiencing the reality they were born into and have manifested for themselves, we only introduce resistance. By worrying about what they do on social media, we only add resistance for ourselves (and displace ourselves from alignment) and for them (push them out of alignment because that puts them into position to resist us in return).

Just think of this as a battle you cannot win. Ask yourself: *Would I rather be right or happy?* Before you answer this question, I want to tell you a story.

> There was a retired colonel, a military man, a man of discipline, who had a teenage son. The son was nothing like his father. The teenage boy liked to wear long hair and baggy pants and ride his skateboard. No matter how much the colonel tried to discipline his son and get him to cut his hair, iron his clothes, and act more disciplined, the

teenager would not comply. The colonel spent months and even years in frustration over his undisciplined son. He just did not know what to do with the boy. So he stayed mad at his son most of the time.

One night, the colonel's son was playing basketball for his high school team when suddenly, in the middle of the game, he collapsed and fell dead to the floor. You see, no one knew until this point that the boy had an undiagnosed heart defect that killed him instantly that evening.

The colonel was devastated. He did not expect this at all. He thought he had a lot of time with his son ahead of him. On the day he buried his teenage boy, he cried inconsolably, mostly for all the time lost in fighting over his boy's clothes and hair. The boy was buried in his favorite baggy pants, with long hair, and with his skateboard. And the colonel thought to himself: *If only I could hold my son one more time, it would not matter what clothes he wore or how long his hair was.*

Often, we spend too much precious time fighting with our kids over things that are not worth fighting about, especially when we have no control over those things, such as their use of electronics or their time spent on social media.

If you ask teenagers how they would feel if their smartphone was taken away, they would answer, "It would feel like my air supply was cut off." And they are not kidding. So taking away their devices to control their use of electronics or limiting their time on social media does not work. It only increases the emotional distance between you and your child. We have already discussed this in other chapters.

Our children and teens often rely on these devices for school and for communicating with friends, classmates, and teachers. They need their devices not only for socializing but also for information.

What You Can Do

We have already established that you cannot control the uncontrollable: your child's choices. However, as the good, loving parent that you are, you can practice the true leader's EEE, as discussed in Step 5 chapter. If you are thinking about your child's activity and safety on social media—if you are concerned about cyberbullying, abusive social media friends, or other dangerous online behaviors—you'll need to elevate, educate, and empower.

Elevate

Tell your children how proud you are of them for being smart and kind to others. Treat your kids (and everyone else in your life) as if they are already the people you want them to be. Remember: if you tell people that they are good, they will eventually prove you right. If you tell them that they are bad, they will eventually prove you right too.

Educate

Teach your children how to be safe on social media, but remember to do this when they are open to hearing you. For this, first catch them in a good mood, or do something with them that puts them in a good mood, such as cooking their favorite meal (that's my weapon of choice, as I love cooking for my family) or doing some activity they enjoy, like playing a game or going on a bike ride—whatever is age-appropriate and fun for them.

Once they are open to talking and hearing you, take advantage and sneak in things to chat about in a by-the-way manner. Keep it light and fun, and try not to sound like you're giving a lecture. Telling a story about someone else, even if you have to make it up, can work great for this purpose. These are the three things you may want to address regarding social media use:

- **Be kind and polite when commenting on others' posts**. Show through example that it's not possible to overcompliment a person. It's better to be nice, so teach kids that the energy that's projected (even via social media) is the energy that will return back.

- **Think twice before posting anything.** Teach your child to think ahead. I told my kids that I have learned from my mentors to think at least two steps ahead when making any decisions. For example, colleges and/or future employers look at your social media profile and may reject you as a candidate if they don't like what they see. Another great strategy to apply is WWGS (What Would Grandma Say?).

- **If you don't know them in person, do not interact with them on social media.** You can set the privacy settings together if your teenager is okay with that, or educate kids on how to do it on their own. And of course, teach them to never share their passwords with anyone.

Empower

Have some faith and trust that you have taught your children well. You cannot be there for the rest of their lives to monitor their behavior and choices, so you must believe in their own power to make wise choices. Inspire your children or teens to be the best human beings they can be. This can be done, again, by elevating them and showing them how much you believe in their goodness, integrity, and strength of character.

Video Games

When it comes to our children and their attachment to video games, the answer is very similar to what we have stated above about social media use. You were born into a place and time very different from your child. The environment that surrounded you during your childhood was very different from the environment surrounding your child today. Remember: your children chose to be born into this time-space reality on purpose, because this is the time-space world where they can manifest what they want to create.

Trying to protect your child from the current exposure (or overexposure, as you may feel) to video games is like saying, "I will teach you the time and place into which I was born, and protect you from the environment into which you were born. I will keep you in the mind-set of the older generations." It's like finding the toys from your childhood and presenting them to your kids while telling them of all the advantages of the old and the dangers of the new world they were born into.

If you think that the games were designed so that our kids would get addicted to them, you've got the cause-and-effect relationship backward. Instead, it starts with our children's desire for the new, which summons the game creators to create the games as the manifestation of our children's desire. In other words, technology is evolving and these games are being created faster and faster because our kids' desire is summoning that creation. This is the basic law of attraction in action.

There have been many books written, films created, and seminars held about this universal law that essentially states that you attract and manifest what you put out into the universe through your thoughts and feelings.

Parents' frustration over video games is often understandable because the new has always annoyed the old, and because the old will never be up to speed with the reality generated by the new. Your children are not trying to control you; it is you who are trying to control them. This is why they will turn away from you and mind their own business: the video game. We as humans naturally turn away from what we cannot control (in this case, your child cannot control you) and gravitate toward the things we can control (in this case, the video game).

You see, it's hard to control humans—they are unpredictable. But machines, like Xbox, iPad, smartphones, PlayStation, and such, *can* be controlled. This is why teenagers would rather attend to a video game than to their parents.

What You Can Do

Find Alignment Within

When you see your child playing video games (again) and it irritates you, just focus on being aware that this is putting you out of alignment with yourself. Your task is to remind yourself that you cannot control another person's behavior (even your own child's), because it only brings you out of alignment. Instead, focus on bringing yourself back into alignment.

Make peace with it and focus on loving and accepting your children just the way they are.

Talk to Your Child

When you have found your alignment, you can admit to your child: "We were born into different times, environments, and even relationships with who we are. Previous generations have been slowing down the new ones, unnecessarily introducing resistance and chaos, but I decided to approach this differently.

"I believe you are a powerful creator with tremendous potential and purpose. It's not my job to dictate to you what that is. You have everything to figure it all out. Your life to you is very different from what my life was to me at your age. I am happy and excited that I got to play my part and you get to play yours. I accept that our parts are different.

"I want you to figure out for yourself how to create and manifest into your experience what you desire. And I will be here to support you whenever you need me."

Try to join them in their game.

Get into the game and accept in advance that you are not going to be as good at it as your child.

What Not to Do

If instead you try to take the video game away, you will see the emotional result of you trying to hold them back, because that's all they are seeing if you resist their natural progress. If parents start putting restrictions on devices, kids will only get sneaky. You will lose their trust, as they will lose yours, too.

There is nothing more disappointing to children than to have someone who loves them not believe in their right to create their own reality. So they withdraw into something that does not judge them (the video game), something that allows them to expand what they seek.

Remember: you cannot love them and worry about them at the same time, because worrying is conditional love. So find a soothing thought that would let you allow them, because you really cannot control them. Love and accept yourself just the way you are, and love and accept your children just the way they are, because you promised yourself that you will feel good no matter how your child behaves.

⊶ ꙮ ꙮ ꙮ ꙯

"Clean Your Room!"

꙯ ꙮ ꙮ ꙮ ⊷

I am sitting in Dr. Ruth's office with Abi, age fourteen.

I was called to join Abi's therapy session because Ruth, Abi's psychologist, wants to address some issues with me—issues that bother me as Abi's mom but over which Abi, as Ruth claims, has no control.

We sit there and discuss Abi's progress at school, her grades, her attitude at home, and her emotional state. Abi has been depressed and anxious, experiencing frequent emotional meltdowns and mental shutdowns. Ruth gives me a quick update on Abi's progress in therapy and asks me if I have any questions.

Feeling overwhelmed, I ask Ruth, "Well, how can I get Abi to clean up her room? Her room is a complete mess. Her clothes are all over the place; her books are mixed with laundry, dirty dishes, small change, some jewelry, and makeup; and it's all just sitting in piles there."

To my surprise, Ruth replied to me with a question: "And what would happen if Abi's room stays messy?"

This question stumbles me for a second as I start to really think. "Well, she cannot find things in this mess."

At this point, Abi enters the conversation: "You mean *you* cannot find things in my room. I know where I put them, so I can find them."

I cannot argue with that, but I try to insist: "But it's not right to live in such a mess!"

Ruth continues, "So tell us: what horrible thing will happen if she does not clean her room? You gave her this room in your house; it's her territory now. How does her mess affect your life? Whose standards are you following when you say that it's not right to live in mess? Are these your standards or your parents' or someone else's?"

***

140

I have to admit, it took me some time (years, to be honest) to really fully understand those words and what they meant, but I get it now. And the affirmation of my new understanding came to me later through the teachings of Abraham through Esther Hicks.

At one of her seminars, a man raised his hand and asked, "What can I do to get my daughter to straighten up her room?"

The reply was, "When parents demand of their children to straighten up their room, what they are really communicating is this: 'I feel better when your room is clean, so I am making my happiness dependent on your behavior.' In return, the children, by not complying with these demands, are responding: 'Oh no! You are supposed to love me unconditionally. I will remind you that when you try to control the uncontrollable (my room's cleanliness, in this case), you get out of alignment with yourself. And I also have to remind you that you need to be loving regardless of conditions, such as my room's state.'"

You see, when we use the external locus of control—meaning that we let factors outside of ourselves (people, events, interactions, political issues, and even weather) have control over how we feel—that puts us in a position of powerlessness. If you remember, when the power to create and control our reality is taken away from us, we feel pain from the loss of expectation, which manifests as anger and frustration with our noncompliant children.

People who try to please you, who comply with your demands, or who change their behavior so that you can feel better are not really helping you grow and evolve. They are not pushing you to look inward and focus on what is really important: your inner alignment.

Sam, for example, who tried very hard to please his parents, grandparents, and teachers (especially in his earlier years, before puberty hit), would go out of his way to be the "golden child," as Abi named him sarcastically. He did not challenge me as much to make me look within myself to find that alignment. Abi, on the other hand, my spirited kid, is in my life for a reason: to teach me some big lessons, including my own alignment, regardless of her behavior or achievements or how messy or clean her room is.

Our spirited children are here to teach us unconditional love, acceptance, kindness (including kindness toward ourselves), and patience (including patience with ourselves).They are here to remind us to stop spending our time and energy trying to control the uncontrollable, which only puts us out of alignment. Instead, they force us focus on the only thing we can control, which is our inner alignment, our relationship with ourselves. Only then does our influence become much more powerful.

***

With all that said, we do have to admit, our children's messy room does affect us too. It's in our house, and we do have a complete right to want that room to be clean and organized. It affects the environmental dimension on your wheel of wellness (Step 3 chapter). However, it's also important to choose your battles.

Let me ask you: what is more important to you: peace and harmony in your relationship with your child or a clean room, which is a constant struggle that sucks the energy and joy out of your life? This is where I like the approach taken by Tamra Skye, my friend and colleague, who has raised a daughter with ADHD—very successfully, I might add. (Tamra wrote the foreword to this book.)

Tamra set very simple and attainable standards when her daughter was a teenager. She did not demand that her daughter's room be kept sparkling clean, but she established very simple rules to maintain the basic safety requirements:

- No biohazard substances. This means that food leftovers could not be left in the room for days to rot.
- There must be a clear path from the door to the bed and from the bed to the window in case of emergency.

That's it!

For ADHD children or teens, this is very doable, especially if they clearly understand the reasoning behind these two rules. In this case, we are not trying to make the child conform to the rules and standards set by other parents, grandparents, teachers, or society. We make new rules that fit our children and keep them safe. Remember: you don't have to make the child fit the rules. You make the rules to fit the child's needs.

***

142

Keep in mind: punishments don't work on ADHD children and teens. If you try to take away things like a smartphone, tablet, or other devices as a form of punishment until they "learn their lesson" or change their behavior, you might be waiting a long time. Abi's dad tried taking away her iPhone in an attempt to control Abi's behavior and make her do what he wanted her to do, including cleaning her room. Needless to say, that did not help their relationship. All it did was make Abi sneak behind his back. It alienated her from her father and damaged their relationship.

ADHD kids are creative and bright, so they quickly come up with a workaround for any given situation, such as losing their smartphone privileges or internet access. At the same time, as we discussed previously, people with ADHD are quite resilient. Their neurodiversity allows them to not dwell on the current situation and lets them quickly move on to the next thought.

* * *

With all that in mind, we can still work with our children on completing some chores, including organizing their room. Here are some tips to help in the process:

1. **Split up the big chore into smaller tasks.** This means don't just tell them to "clean their room." Instead, break up this seemingly unfathomable chore into smaller tasks and have your child do only one task at a time. Here is a list of tasks you can use for cleaning and organizing a room. Kids only have to complete one at a time, and when they do, praise and thank them!
   - Collect all the trash into a bag or a box and discard it.
   - Collect all the dirty clothes into a laundry basket.
   - Collect all the things that belong in other rooms (that do not belong in this room) and remove them from the room.
   - Put away things that are on the floor—or at least pick them up.
   - Put away everything that is on the dresser or night stand.
   - Put away things that are on the desk.

   You can come up with your own list of items and make the tasks as small as you want based on your child's age and developmental stage. They don't have to be all done back to back or even on the same day. Allow time for each task and praise, praise, praise!

2. **Make it fun.** For younger kids especially (but it works with older children too), you can turn room organizing into a game. You can still break up the big chore into smaller tasks, but you can make it playful. For example:
   - Pick up everything that's red.
   - Pick up everything that's blue.
   - Pick up everything that's soft.
   - Pick up everything that's round.

   Keep in mind, however, that after each completed task, you must reward your child with at least a "Thank you!" or "Great job!"

3. **Keep your sense of humor.** Keep it light and fun, if you can help it. You don't always have to win 100 percent in this game of chores. Find the middle ground and focus on loving and accepting your children for who they are—magnificent, wonderful, wild, and free human beings. That's what made them come into this world with ADHD. With ADHD, they don't have to conform to everyone's rules; they can just make their own. Become your child's greatest advocate and cheerleader, and you will see how much your relationship changes for the better.

Additional Bonus:
Parent's Resource Guide
to ADHD

The Dos and Don'ts:
What Your ADHD Kid Wishes You Knew

The ADHD brain moves faster than regular brains, which makes it very special, talented, creative, and quick. Sometimes, ADHD kids' brakes and filters cannot keep up with their fast-moving brains, which causes social discord and issues at school. It's up to us, as parents, to become our kids' greatest supporters and advocates.

This cheat sheet is here to help you with the most common dos and don'ts. This list was inspired by actual children, teens, and adults who have ADHD. This is what they want you to know.

Don't do this	Do this instead
Don't say: "I know how you feel. I get distracted sometimes too." Unless you also have ADHD, you really don't know how they feel.	Instead say: "I don't know how you feel, but I will help you in any way I can." This tells kids that you have their back and they can count on your support.
Don't say: "This medication will fix what's wrong with you." This makes kids feel like they need to be fixed. It hurts their self-esteem.	Instead say: "This medication is a tool that can help you make the most out of your strengths. Sometimes, your brain is supercharged and needs to slow down." Not everyone uses the medication, and there are many other ways to manage ADHD symptoms.
Don't say: "You don't have to tell others that you have ADHD." This may cause your child to feel ashamed of it.	Instead you may say: "It's up to you if you want to tell others that you have ADHD." This is a big part of who they are, and there is nothing to be ashamed of.

Don't say: "Just calm down" or "Relax" when your child/teen feels agitated or excited.	Instead:
	• Avoid or prevent emotional meltdowns before they escalate.
Individuals should be allowed to express themselves.	• Hand your child a snow globe and suggest shaking it and staring at it; this is very relaxing to an ADHD brain. After your child calms down, discuss feelings in a calm way.
	• Try a weighted blanket to control anxiety: "It feels like a hug!"
	• Pet therapy and music therapy also work great.
	• Being in the natural environment can be calming and therapeutic.

Don't say "You need to act normal." What is *normal*, anyway?	Instead:
	• Say "I love you" as frequently as you can.
	• If your child is frustrated, ask, "Do you want to talk about it?" to provide an outlet.
	• Become your child's advocate at school.

Don't force your child to focus and concentrate on homework and complete it all in one sitting. Don't expect your ADHD child to sit and work on the homework until it's done.	• Do allow your child to play and work off some extra energy after school before sitting down for homework. • Do give your child frequent breaks and rewards for tasks completed. • Have your child stand on one leg while completing a worksheet or sit on an exercise ball while studying.
To your child, this is an impossible torture, as it is to you.	• Give your child a stress ball or a small hand toy to fiddle with while reading. • Let your child doodle on note pages.
Don't say/yell, "Why do I have to repeat myself a dozen times?!" Saying the same thing over and over again does not help or change anything.	Instead, try acting. If your child is not responding to your voice, come up and touch your child on the shoulder. If your teen does not respond to your text, send another text.
Don't say "How could you forget that?!"	• Write (on a Post-it) or text your child reminders (more than once) and offer to send a reminder text. • Put *everything* on the calendar. Post reminders in as many places as possible. • Write lists and teach kids to write task lists for themselves.

If your child is fixated on something, don't refuse to find out about it.	Instead say "I will check it out" and really follow through.
Don't fight about chores and procrastination. To an ADHD child, brain chores are boring, sometimes impossible endeavors.	Instead, break down big tasks, such as "clean your room," into smaller tasks, and reward your child for completing each task. The ADHD brain needs novelty, challenges, and deadlines. So make these tasks fun. Turn them into a game.
Don't say "It's like you are not even trying!" People with ADHD who say they are trying are trying more than you can imagine.	Instead, encourage your child every step of the way.
Don't use punishment as a mode of discipline. It works with compliant kids without ADHD.	Instead, use gamification, encouragement, and rewards as the best way to get your child to do what you need. Discipline (taking away things or sending kids to their room) does not work on ADHD kids. They simply will redirect their attention to something they can do or control.
Don't be an enabler by doing things for your child. Do not bring forgotten homework to school	Kids might appreciate your help in the moment, but in the long run, they will feel incompetent, and you will end up feeling resentful. Communicate with your ADHD child honestly.

About the Author

Gelena Gorelik, MS, RD, is a certified advanced level Strategic Intervention coach specializing in relationship coaching for parents of children and teenagers with ADHD. Gelena received her training at the Institute for Strategic Intervention, which uses methods developed by Anthony Robbins and Chloe Madanes.

Coach Gelena holds a master of science degree from the University of California, Davis. She is a Registered Dietitian and a lifelong educator who has dedicated her career and passion to the development of the minds of young adults. She has developed curricula for college courses, professional seminars, and workshops presented at state and national conferences.

Today the mom of a teenager with ADHD, Gelena helps other parents of teens find new peace and harmony in their family dynamics. To learn more about Coach Gelena's approach, find out about available courses and webinars, or schedule a personal coaching session with Coach Gelena, please visit www.coachgelena.com or www.BayAreaHappinessCoach.com.

Printed in the United States
By Bookmasters

Printed in the United States
By Bookmasters